Perusals

Note to the reader: Except for names of specific persons, places or things, words typically have _several meanings_. The **gloss** of a word in bold face here offers _only_ the word's meaning in context.

gloss – a brief marginal note explaining a difficult word

Aerie Press
28 Patriot Street
North Andover MA 01845

Editor: John Willard, Donald St. John, Peter Beaven

Contributor: Nikhil Deliwala

Version 5 – November, 2022

Published by
The Cheshire Press
an imprint of The Cheshire Group
Andover, MA 01810
www.cheshirepress.com

ISBN: 978-0-9987465-4-8

Library of Congress: 2017945201

Printed in the United States of America

Beaven & Associates
3 Dundee Park, #202 A
Andover, MA 01810
978-475-5487
www.beavenandassociates.com

Perusals

The word anthology comes to us from the Classical Greek anthos meaning flowers, and logia meaning collection. In time this collection came to be a selection of poems, wise sayings, stories, essays, and chronicles from history. Today as a selection of such writings, Perusals, edited by John Willard, invites the reader of all ages to explore short examples of the works of the great and eloquent thinkers from over the centuries. Thus the armchair traveler can learn from the ideas expressed by Socrates in ancient Greece to those of Einstein in modern America. At his fingertips, the reader of Perusals discovers if his interpretations yield a proper understanding of the diverse and demanding material, especially if he avails himself of the penetrating questions that appear in exercises that follow each selection. By the same means, the pragmatic student facing a standardized test can test his wits and learn to score and rank his ability to handle demanding passages. Both the venturesome explorer and conscientious student may wish to continue to the next books in the series, Perspectives I, which focuses on literature, and Perspectives II, on history.

Table of Contents

Fiction

Table of Contents

Nonfiction

Albert Einstein's Letter to FDR (1939)

Letter from German physicist Albert Einstein, Nobelist and acknowledged genius, to President Franklin D. Roosevelt about the possible construction of nuclear bombs – an undertaking that went forward as the Manhattan Project. It led to the obliteration of the Japanese cities Hiroshima and Nagasaki and, shortly thereafter, Japan's surrender, ending WWII.

Old Grove Rd.
Nassau Point
Peconic, Long Island

August 2nd, 1939

F.D. Roosevelt
President of the United States
White House
Washington, D.C.

Sir:

Some recent work by **E. Fermi** and **L. Szilard**, which has been communicated to me in **manuscript**, leads me to expect that the element uranium may be turned into a new and important source of energy in the immediate future. Certain aspects of the situation which has arisen seem to call for watchfulness and, if necessary, quick action on the part of the administration. I believe therefore that it is my duty to bring to your attention the following facts and recommendations:

In the course of the last four months it has been made probable -- through the work of **Joliot** in France as well as Fermi and Szilard in America -- that it may become possible to set up a nuclear chain reaction in a large mass of uranium, by which vast amounts of power and large quantities of new radium like elements would be generated. Now it appears almost certain that this could be achieved in the immediate future.

Enrico Fermi – Italian physicist who worked on first nuclear reactor

Leo Szilard – Hungarian-American physicist who co-wrote this letter

manuscript – any document written by hand versus being printed or reproduced in some other way

Frederic Joliot-Curie – French physicist who, with his Polish wife Marie, won the Nobel prize for their work on radioactive elements

5

This new phenomenon would also lead to the construction of bombs, and it is conceivable -- though much less certain -- that extremely powerful bombs of a new type may thus be constructed. A single bomb of this type, carried by boat and exploded in a port, might very well destroy the whole port together with some of the surrounding territory. However, such bombs might very well prove to be too heavy for transportation by air.

The United States has only very poor ores of uranium in moderate quantities. There is some good ore in Canada and the former **Czechoslovakia**, while the most important source of uranium is **Belgian Congo**.

In view of this situation you may think it desirable to have some permanent contact maintained between the Administration and the group of physicists working on **chain reactions** in America. One possible way of achieving this might be for you to entrust with this task a person who has your confidence and who could perhaps serve in an unofficial capacity. His task might comprise the following:

a) To approach Government Departments, keep them informed of the further development, and put forward recommendations for Government action, giving particular attention to the problem of uranium ore for the United States;

b) To speed up the experimental work, which is at present being carried on within the limits of the budgets of University laboratories, by providing funds, if such funds be required, through his contacts with private persons who are willing to make a contribution for this cause, and perhaps also by obtaining the co-operation of industrial laboratories which have the necessary equipment.

I understand that Germany has actually stopped the sale of uranium from the Czechoslovakian mines, which she

Czechoslovakia – as of 1993 the Czech Republic and Slovakia

Belgian Congo – Belgium's African colony 1908-1960; now the Democratic Republic of the Congo

chain reaction – a series of nuclear fissions in which neutrons released by splitting one atom led to the splitting of others, producing energy

has taken over. That she should have taken such early action might perhaps be understood on the ground that the son of the German Under-Secretary of State, von Weizsäcker, is attached to the Kaiser Wilhelm Institute in Berlin where some of the American work on uranium is now being repeated.

Yours very truly,

(Albert Einstein)

Albert Einstein's Letter to FDR

1. The letter is being sent from:
    A. Germany
    B. New York
    C. New Jersey

2. The letter is posted from:
    A. before the war
    B. in mid-war
    C. near the war's end

3. The physicist couple working with radioactive materials is:
    A. Szilards
    B. Fermis
    C. Curies

4. The letter suggests the bomb is most feasibly delivered by:
    A. air
    B. sea
    C. land

5. The reason a potential bomb might not be deliverable by plane is the bomb's potential:
    A. explosive nature
    B. volatility
    C. weight

6. The best source of uranium is said to be:
    A. Africa
    B. Czechoslovakia
    C. Eastern Europe

7. Uranium is said to be no longer obtainable from:
    A. Africa
    B. Czechoslovakia
    C. Eastern Europe

8. Close contact is urged between the administration and:
    A. physicists
    B. the United States
    C. industrial laboratories

9. American work on uranium is said to be duplicated at an institute in:
    A. Germany
    B. England
    C. Hungary

10. The word *"capacity"* as used in ¶ 5 most nearly means:
    A. great size
    B. role
    C. volume

The Burning of Washington
Dolley Madison (1814)

Excerpt from a letter by First Lady Dolley Madison to her sister, Anna, written the day before Washington, D.C. was burned by British forces during the War of 1812. The letter describes the abandonment of the White House and Mrs. Madison's famous actions saving artist Gilbert Stuart's priceless portrait of George Washington. As Mrs. Madison fled, she **rendezvoused** with her husband, and together, from a safe distance, they watched Washington burn.

My husband left me yesterday morning to join General Winder. He inquired anxiously whether I had courage or firmness to remain in the President's house until his return on the morrow, or succeeding day, and on my assurance that I had no fear but for him, and the success of our army, he left, **beseeching** me to take care of myself, and of the Cabinet papers, public and private. I have since received two **dispatches** from him, written with a pencil. The last is alarming, because he desires I should be ready at a moment's warning to enter my carriage, and leave the city; that the enemy seemed stronger than had at first been reported, and it might happen that they would reach the city with the intention of destroying it. I am accordingly ready; I have pressed as many Cabinet papers into trunks as to fill one carriage; our private property must be sacrificed, as it is impossible to **procure** wagons for its transportation. I am determined not to go myself until I see Mr. Madison safe, so that he can accompany me, as I hear of much hostility towards him. **Disaffection** stalks around us. My friends and acquaintances are all gone, even Colonel C. with his hundred, who were stationed as a guard in this inclosure. French John (a faithful servant), with his usual activity and resolution, offers to **spike the cannon** at the gate, and lay a train of powder, which would blow up the British, should they enter the house. To the last proposition I positively object, without being able to make him understand why all advantages in war may not be taken.

Wednesday Morning, twelve o'clock. -- Since sunrise I have been turning my **spy-glass** in every direction, and watching with unwearied anxiety, hoping to discover the approach of

rendezvous (Fr.) – meeting at an agreed time and place, typically between two people

beseech – urgently ask, request, implore
dispatches – written messages, particularly official communication, sent with speed

procure – obtain, provide
disaffection – a state of dissatisfaction or alienation
spike a cannon – to hammer a nail into the weapon to prevent it from firing

spy-glass – small telescope

9

my dear husband and his friends; but, alas! I can **descry** only groups of military, wandering in all directions, as if there was a lack of arms, or of spirit to fight for their own fireside.

Three o'clock. -- Will you believe it, my sister? we have had a battle, or **skirmish**, near Bladensburg, and here I am still, within sound of the cannon! Mr. Madison comes not. May God protect us! Two messengers, covered with dust, come to bid me **fly**; but here I mean to wait for him... At this late hour a wagon has been procured, and I have had it filled with **plate** and the most valuable portable articles, belonging to the house. Whether it will reach its destination, the "Bank of Maryland," or fall into the hands of British soldiery, events must determine. Our kind friend, Mr. Carroll, has come to hasten my departure, and in a very bad **humor** with me, because I insist on waiting until the large picture of General Washington is secured, and it requires to be unscrewed from the wall. This process was found too **tedious** for these perilous moments; I have ordered the frame to be broken, and the canvas taken out. It is done! and the precious portrait placed in the hands of two gentlemen of New York, for safe keeping. And now, dear sister, I must leave this house, or the retreating army will make me a prisoner in it by filling up the road I am directed to take. When I shall again write to you, or where I shall be to-morrow, I cannot tell!

descry – discern, see

skirmish – brief period or encounter of fighting

fly – escape, flee
plate – dishes, cutlery, etc., made of gold or silver

humor – mood, state of mind

tedious – tiresome or causing fatigue

The Burning of Washington

1. The U.S. president at the time of the assault is:
    A. Adams
    B. Madison
    C. Jackson

2. The letter is posted to the writer's:
    A. spouse
    B. sister
    C. Congressman

3. According to the excerpt, the woman has been urged to depart with:
    A. only herself and staff
    B. their private property
    C. Cabinet documents

4. The woman is alone in the White House except for:
    A. a servant
    B. her children
    C. a military guard

5. Before fleeing, the woman hopes she herself can:
    A. spike the cannon
    B. set a trail of gunpowder
    C. neither A nor B

6. At the last moments the woman fears that:
    A. her husband might be dead
    B. her servant will be too late
    C. she may be captured

7. The woman is still tarrying at 3 p.m. to:
    A. rescue a painting
    B. await her husband's arrival
    C. both A & B

8. On Wednesday morning the woman anxiously uses a spy-glass to detect the coming of:
    A. enemy soldiers
    B. her husband
    C. more wagons

9. Two dusty messengers arrive:
    A. with news of the president
    B. to urge her to flee
    C. to secure the painting of George Washington

10. The word *beseech* as used in ¶ 2 most nearly means:
    A. warn
    B. plead
    C. threaten

Canterbury Tales: Prologue`
Geoffrey Chaucer (1387-1400)

This is a <u>Modern English</u> version of the **Middle English** original. The tales are recounted by 20 pilgrims on their way to Canterbury Cathedral, site of the 1170 martyrdom of Saint Thomas à Beckett, an archbishop killed at the hands of four knights of King Henry II, acting on behalf of the king. Henry had appointed former comrade Beckett to the post and in the end regretted the appointment as much as the priest's murder.

When April with his showers sweet with fruit

The drought of March has pierced unto the root

And bathed each **vein** with **liquor** that has power

To generate therein and **sire** the flower;

When **Zephyr** also has, with his sweet breath,

Quickened again, in every **holt** and **heath**,

The tender shoots and buds, and the young sun

Into the **Ram** one half his course has run,

And many little birds make melody

That sleep through all the night with open eye

(So Nature pricks them on to ramp and rage) -

Then do folk long to go on pilgrimage,

And **palmers** to go seeking out strange **strands**,

To distant shrines well known in **sundry** lands.

And specially from every **shire**'s end

Of England they to Canterbury wend,

Geoffrey Chaucer – known as the Father of English literature, considered the greatest English poet of the Middle Ages

Middle English – in use from the 12th to 15th century. Writings and speech of later writers are in Modern English

vein – stem, capillary
liquor – liquid (water)
sire – give birth to
Zephyr – the West Wind
quicken – bring to life
holt – grove, wood
heath – uncultivated land
Ram – the sign of Aries in the astrology-based calendar – the sun here is halfway in its annual course

palmer – pilgrim, identified by wearing of a palm leaf
strands – beaches, coasts
sundry – miscellaneous, various
shire – county (Brit.)

The holy blessed martyr there to seek

Who helped them when they lay so ill and weak.

Befell that, in that season, on a day

In Southwark, at the **Tabard**, as I lay

Ready to start upon my pilgrimage

To Canterbury, full of devout **homage**,

There came at nightfall to that **hostelry**

Some nine and twenty in a company

Of sundry persons who had chanced to **fall**

In fellowship, and pilgrims were they all

That toward Canterbury town would ride.

The rooms and stables spacious were and wide,

And well we there were eased, and of the best.

And briefly, when the sun had gone to rest,

So had I spoken with them, every one,

That I was of their fellowship **anon**,

And made agreement that we'd early rise

To take the road, as you I will **apprise**.

But none the less, whilst I have time and space,

Before yet farther in this tale I pace,

It seems to me accordant with reason

befell – (it) happened

Tabard – the inn where the travelers have been put up

homage – respect or reverence paid, praise

hostelry – hotel providing overnight lodging for travelers

fall in fellowship – get acquainted, become companions

anon – soon

apprise – inform

13

To inform you of the state of every one

Of all of these, as it appeared to me,

And who they were, and what was their **degree**,

And even how **arrayed** there at the inn;

And with a knight thus will I first begin.

degree – social station or rank

arrayed – distributed, arranged, housed

Canterbury Tales: Prologue

1. The original Prologue is written in this English:
   - A. Old
   - B. Middle
   - C. Early modern

2. There are roughly this many assembled pilgrims:
   - A. 20
   - B. 30
   - C. 40

3. The pilgrims are headed to:
   - A. the court of Henry II
   - B. London
   - C. Canterbury

4. Towards the end of the passage, the narrator begins to describe all of the following *except* each pilgrim's:
   - A. position in the society
   - B. age
   - C. housing arrangement at the inn

5. The pilgrims are traveling:
   - A. on horseback
   - B. on foot
   - C. in a procession led by priests

6. The pilgrimage is taking place in:
   - A. early summer
   - B. March
   - C. April

7. The first tale is to be related by:
   - A. the host of the Tabard
   - B. a knight
   - C. a palmer

8. The narrator is apparently a:
   - A. poet
   - B. physician
   - C. one of the arriving pilgrims

9. Before the pilgrims set out from the Tabard, the narrator first plans to:
   - A. describe each one
   - B. pray for their safe journey
   - C. record each pilgrim's name and origin

10. The term *"sundry"* (¶ 1&2) used here most nearly means:
   - A. sunburned
   - B. temperate
   - C. various

Captain Murderer
Charles Dickens (1860)

If we all knew our own minds (in a more enlarged sense than the popular acceptation of that phrase), I suspect we should find our nurses responsible for most of the dark corners we are forced to go back to, against our wills.

The first **diabolical** character who intruded himself on my peaceful youth was a certain Captain Murderer. This wretch must have been an offshoot of the **Blue Beard** family, but I had no suspicion of the **consanguinity** in those times. His warning name would seem to have awakened no general prejudice against him, for he was admitted into the best society and possessed immense wealth. Captain Murderer's mission was matrimony, and the gratification of a cannibal appetite with tender brides. On his marriage morning, he always caused both sides of the way to church to be planted with curious flowers; and when his bride said, "Dear Captain Murderer, I never saw flowers like these before: what are they called?" he answered, "They are called **Garnish** for house-lamb," and laughed at his ferocious practical joke in a horrid manner, disquieting the minds of the noble bridal company, with a very sharp show of teeth, then displayed for the first time. He made love in a coach and six, and married in a coach and twelve, and all his horses were milk-white horses with one red spot on the back which he caused to be hidden by the harness. For, the spot *would* come there, though every horse was milk-white when Captain Murderer bought him. And the spot was young bride's blood. (*To this terrific point I am indebted for my personal experience of a shudder and cold beads on the forehead.*) When Captain Murderer had made an end of feasting and revelry, and had dismissed the noble guests, and was alone with his wife on the day month after their marriage, it was his whimsical custom to produce a golden rolling-pin and a silver **pie-board**. Now, there was this special feature in the Captain's courtships, that he always asked if the young lady could make pie-crust; and if she couldn't by nature or education, she was taught. Well. When the bride saw Captain Murderer produce the golden rolling-pin and silver pie-board, she remembered this, and turned up her laced-silk sleeves to make a pie. The Captain brought out

Charles Dickens – well-loved Victorian England novelist and social critic

diabolical – devilish, fiendish

Blue Beard – folktale of a violent nobleman in the habit of serially murdering his wives

consanguinity – blood relation, kinship, close affinity

garnish – decorative or flavorful touch to a dish

pie-board – kitchen cutting board

16

a silver pie-dish of immense capacity, and the Captain brought out flour and butter and eggs and all things needful, except the inside of the pie; of materials for the **staple** of the pie itself, the Captain brought out none. Then said the lovely bride, "Dear Captain Murderer, what pie is this to be?" He replied, "A meat pie." Then said the lovely bride, "Dear Captain Murderer, I see no meat." The Captain humorously retorted, "Look in the glass." She looked in the glass, but still she saw no meat, and then the Captain roared with laughter, and suddenly frowning and drawing his sword, bade her roll out the crust. So she rolled out the crust, dropping large tears upon it all the time because he was so cross, and when she had lined the dish with crust and had cut the crust all ready to fit the top, the Captain called out, "*I* see the meat in the glass!" And the bride looked up at the glass, just in time to see the Captain cutting her head off; and he chopped her in pieces, and peppered her, and salted her, and put her in the pie, and sent it to the baker's, and ate it all, and picked the bones.

Captain Murderer went on in this way, prospering exceedingly, until he came to choose a bride from two twin sisters, and at first didn't know which to choose. For, though one was fair and the other dark, they were both equally beautiful. But the fair twin loved him, and the dark twin hated him, so he chose the fair one. The dark twin would have prevented the marriage if she could, but she couldn't; however, on the night before it, much suspecting Captain Murderer, she **stole out** and climbed his garden wall, and looked in at his window through a chink in the shutter, and saw him having his teeth filed sharp. Next day she listened all day, and heard him make his joke about the house-lamb. And that day month, he had the paste rolled out, and cut the fair twin's head off, and chopped her in pieces, and peppered her, and salted her, and put her in the pie, and sent it to the baker's, and ate it all, and picked the bones.

Now, the dark twin had had her suspicions much increased by the filing of the Captain's teeth, and again by the house-lamb joke. Putting all things together when he gave out that her sister was dead, she **divined** the truth, and determined to be

staple – main or routine ingredient

stole out – went secretly, exited in a concealed or unobserved manner

divined – discerned, intuited, guessed

revenged. So, she went up to Captain Murderer's house, and knocked at the knocker and pulled at the bell, and when the Captain came to the door, said: "Dear Captain Murderer, marry me next for I always loved you and was jealous of my sister." The Captain took it as a compliment, and made a polite answer, and the marriage was quickly arranged. On the night before it, the bride again climbed to his window, and again saw him having his teeth filed sharp. At this sight she laughed such a terrible laugh at the chink in the shutter, that the Captain's blood **curdled**, and he said: "I hope nothing has disagreed with me!" At that, she laughed again, a still more terrible laugh, and the shutter was opened and search made, but she was nimbly gone, and there was no one. Next day they went to church in a coach and twelve, and were married. And that day month, she rolled the pie-crust out, and Captain Murderer cut her head off, and chopped her in pieces, and peppered her, and salted her, and put her in the pie, and sent it to the baker's, and ate it all, and picked the bones.

But before she began to roll out the paste she had taken a deadly poison of a most awful character, distilled from toads' eyes and spiders' knees; and Captain Murderer had hardly picked her last bone, when he began to swell, and to turn blue, and to be all over spots, and to scream. And he went on swelling and turning bluer, and being more all over spots and screaming, until he reached from floor to ceiling and from wall to wall; and then, at one o'clock in the morning, he blew up with a loud explosion. At the sound of it, all the milk-white horses in the stables broke their halters and went mad, and then they galloped over everybody in Captain Murderer's house (beginning with the family blacksmith who had filed his teeth) until the whole were dead, and then they galloped away.

curdled – congealed, coagulated, formed into lumps

Captain Murderer

1. The Captain's "house-lamb" is:
    A. a dog
    B. flowers
    C. human flesh

2. The reflection in the mirror ("glass") is:
    A. the pie filling
    B. the Captain's teeth
    C. the flour, butter and eggs

3. The married couple make love in a:
    A. castle
    B. coach
    C. kitchen

4. A specific job of the blacksmith is to file:
    A. hooves
    B. horseshoes
    C. teeth

5. This finally ends the Captain's life:
    A. an explosion
    B. a poison potion
    C. a stabbing

6. One twin's suspicion is confirmed when:
    A. the Captain roars with laughter
    B. she looks up at a mirror
    C. she sees the Captain have his teeth filed sharp

7. The milk-white horses go mad at the sound of:
    A. the dark twin's terrible laugh
    B. the Captain's screams
    C. a stomach bursting

8. By the end of narrative:
    A. everyone is dead
    B. only the dark twin survives
    C. the blacksmith survives

9. This type of story is best classified as a:
    A. grim fairy tale
    B. fable
    C. moral lesson story

10. The word "*divined*" (¶ 3) as used in the passage most nearly means:
    A. prayed
    B. invented
    C. inferred

The Celebrated Jumping Frog of Calaveras County
Mark Twain, pen name of Samuel Clemens (1865)

In compliance with the request of a friend of mine, who wrote me from the East, I called on good-natured, **garrulous** old Simon Wheeler, and inquired after my friend's friend, Leonidas W. Smiley, as requested to do, and I hereunto append the result. I have a lurking suspicion that Leonidas W. Smiley is a myth; that my friend never knew such a personage; and that he only **conjectured** that, if I asked old Wheeler about him, it would remind him of his **infamous** Jim Smiley, and he would go to work and bore me nearly to death with some **infernal reminiscence** of him as long and tedious as it should be useless to me. If that was the design, it certainly succeeded.

I found Simon Wheeler dozing comfortably by the bar-room stove of the old, **dilapidated** tavern in the ancient mining camp of Angel's, and I noticed that he was fat and bald-headed, and had an expression of **winning** gentleness and simplicity upon his tranquil **countenance**. He roused up and gave me good-day. I told him a friend of mine had commissioned me to make some inquiries about a cherished companion of his boyhood named Leonidas W. Smiley — Rev. Leonidas W. Smiley, a young minister of the Gospel, who he had heard was at one time a resident of Angel's Camp. I added that, if Mr. Wheeler could tell me any thing about this Rev. Leonidas W. Smiley, I would feel under many obligations to him.

Simon Wheeler backed me into a corner and blockaded me there with his chair, and then sat me down and reeled off the monotonous narrative which follows this paragraph. He never smiled, he never frowned, he never changed his voice from the gentle-flowing key to which he tuned the initial sentence, he never **betrayed** the slightest suspicion of enthusiasm; but all through the **interminable** narrative there ran a vein of impressive earnestness and sincerity, which showed me plainly that, so far from his imagining that there was anything ridiculous or funny about his story, he regarded it as a really important matter, and admired its two heroes as men of **transcendent** genius in **finesse**. To me, the spectacle of a

Calaveras – county located in the heart of California Gold Country
garrulous – tiresomely talkative

conjectured – guessed, surmised
infamous – notorious, with a bad reputation
infernal – damnable
reminiscence – recollection
dilapidated – deteriorated through neglect, in disrepair
winning – pleasing, attractive
countenance – face

betrayed – revealed
interminable – tiresomely long

20

man drifting serenely along through such a queer **yarn** without ever smiling, was exquisitely absurd. As I said before, I asked him to tell me what he knew of Rev. Leonidas W. Smiley, and he replied as follows. I let him go on in his own way, and never interrupted him once: There was a feller here once by the name of Jim Smiley, in the winter of '49 or may be it was the spring of '50 I don't recollect exactly, somehow, though what makes me think it was one or the other is because I remember the big **flume** wasn't finished when he first came to the camp; but any way, he was the **curiosest** man about always betting on any thing that turned up you ever see, if he could get any body to bet on the other side; and if he couldn't, he'd change sides. Any way that suited the other man would suit him any way just so's he got a bet, he was satisfied. But still he was lucky, **uncommon** lucky; he most always come out winner. He was always ready and laying for a chance; there couldn't be no **solittry** thing mentioned but that **feller'd** offer to bet on it, and -take any side you please, as I was just telling you. If there was a horse-race, you'd find him **flush**, or you'd find him busted at the end of it; if there was a dog-fight, he'd bet on it; if there was a cat-fight, he'd bet on it; if there was a chicken-fight, he'd bet on it; why, if there was two birds setting on a fence, he would bet you which one would fly first; or if there was a **camp-meeting**, he would be there reg'lar, to bet on Parson Walker, which he judged to be the best **exhorter** about here, and so he was, too, and a good man. If he even seen a **straddle-bug** start to go anywheres, he would bet you how long it would take him to get wherever he was going to, and if you took him up, he would **foller** that straddle-bug to Mexico but what he would find out where he was bound for and how long he was on the road. Lots of the boys here has seen that Smiley, and can tell you about him. Why, it never made no difference to him he would bet on any thing the **dangdest** feller. Parson Walker's wife laid very sick once, for a good while, and it seemed as if they **warn's** going to save her; but one morning he come in, and Smiley asked how she was, and he said she was considerable better thank the Lord for his **inftnit** mercy and coming on so smart that, with the blessing of **Providence**, she'd get well yet; and Smiley, before he

transcendent – surpassing
finesse – adroitness, skill
yarn – tale, story

flume – man-made channel for flowing water
curiosest – strangest, oddest

uncommon – unusually
solittry – single, solitary
feller – fellow, guy
flush – having plenty of money

camp-meeting – outdoor religious meeting
exhort – strongly urge
straddle-bug – long-legged insect
foller – follow

dangdest – damnedest
warn's – weren't

inftnit – infinite

thought, says, "Well, I'll risk two-and-a-half that she don't, any way."

Thish-yer Smiley had a mare the boys called her the fifteen-minute **nag**, but that was only in fun, you know, because, of course, she was faster than that and he used to win money on that horse, for all she was so slow and always had the asthma, or the **distemper**, or the **consumption**, or something of that kind. They used to give her two or three hundred yards start, and then pass her under way; but always at the fag-end of the race she'd get excited and desperate-like, and come **cavorting** and **straddling up**, and scattering her legs around limber, sometimes in the air, and sometimes out to one side amongst the fences, and kicking up m-o-r-e dust, and raising m-o-r-e racket with her coughing and sneezing and blowing her nose and always **fetch up** at the stand just about a neck ahead, as near as you could **cipher** it down.

And he had a little small bull pup, that to look at him you'd think he wan's worth a cent, but to set around and look **ornery**, and lay for a chance to steal something. But as soon as money was up on him, he was a different dog; his underjaw'd begin to stick out like the **fo'castle** of a steamboat, and his teeth would uncover, and shine savage like the furnaces. And a dog might tackle him, and bully-rag him, and bite him, and throw him over his shoulder two or three times, and Andrew Jackson which was the name of the pup Andrew Jackson would never let on but what he was satisfied, and hadn't expected nothing else and the bets being doubled and doubled on the other side all the time, till the money was all up; and then all of a sudden he would grab that other dog jest by the j'int of his hind leg and freeze on it not chew, you understand, but only jest grip and hang on till they **thronged up the sponge**, if it was a year. Smiley always come out winner on that pup, till he harnessed a dog once that didn't have no hind legs, because they'd been sawed off by a circular saw, and when the thing had gone along far enough, and the money was looked sorter discouraged-like, and didn't try no more to win the fight, and so he got shucked out bad. He give Smiley a look, as much as to say his heart was broke, and it was his fault, for putting up all up, and he come to make a

Providence – divine guidance

thish-yer – this (here)
nag – old worn-out horse

distemper – viral animal disease
consumption – lung disease
cavorting – prancing, gamboling, jumping
straddling up – sprawling
fetch up – come to a rest
cipher down – discern, figure out

ornery – stubborn, bad-tempered
forecastle – raised deck at the bow of a ship

throng up the sponge – threw in the towel, gave up

22

snatch for his pet bolt, he saw in a minute how he'd been imposed on, and how the other dog had him in the door, so to speak, and he 'peered surprised, and then he a dog that hadn't no hind legs for him to take bolt of, which was his main dependence in a fight, and then he limped off a **piece** and laid down and died. It was a good pup, was that Andrew Jackson, and would have made a name for hisself if he'd lived, for the stuff was in him, and he had genius I know it, because he hadn't had no opportunities to speak of, and it don't stand to reason that a dog could make such a fight as he could under them circumstances, if he hadn't no talent. It always makes me feel sorry when I think of that last fight of his'n, and the way it turned out.

Well, thish-yer Smiley had rat-tarriers, and chicken cocks, and tom-cats, and all of them kind of things, till you couldn't rest, and you couldn't fetch nothing for him to bet on but he'd match you. He ketched a frog one day, and took him home, and said he cal'klated to edercate him; and so he never done nothing for three months but set in his back yard and **learn** that frog to jump. And you bet you he did learn him, too. He'd give him a little punch behind, and the next minute you'd see that frog whirling in the air like a doughnut see him turn one **summerset**, or may be a couple, if he got a good start, and come down flat-footed and all right, like a cat. He got him up so in the matter of catching flies, and kept him in practice so constant, that he'd nail a fly every time as far as he could see him. Smiley said all a frog wanted was education, and he could do most any thing and I believe him. Why, I've seen him set Dan'l Webster down here on this floor Dan'l Webster was the name of the frog and sing out, "Flies, Dan'l, flies!" and quicker'n you could wink, he'd spring straight up, and snake a fly off'n the counter there, and flop down on the floor again as solid as a gob of mud, and fall to scratching the side of his head with his hind foot as indifferent as if he hadn't no idea he'd been doin' any more'n any frog might do. You never see a frog so modest and straightforward as he was, for all he was so gifted. And when it come to fair and square jumping on a dead level, he could get over more ground at one straddle than any animal of his breed you ever see. Jumping on a dead level was his strong suit, you understand; and when

snatch for his pet bolt – grab his pet's leg

a piece – a distance, awhile

learn – teach

summerset – somersault

23

it come to that, Smiley would ante up money on him as long as he had **a red**. Smiley was monstrous proud of his frog, and well he might be, for fellers that had traveled and been everywheres, all said he laid over any frog that ever they see.

red – (red copper) cent

Well, Smiley kept the beast in a little lattice box, and he used to fetch him down town sometimes and lay for a bet. One day a feller a stranger in the camp, he was come across him with his box, and says:

"What might it be that you've got in the box?"

And Smiley says, sorter indifferent like, "It might be a parrot, or it might be a canary, may be, but it an't it's only just a frog."

And the feller took it, and looked at it careful, and turned it round this way and that, and says, "H'm so 'tis. Well, what's he good for?"

"Well," Smiley says, easy and careless, "He's good enough for one thing, I should judge he can outjump any frog in Calaveras county."

The feller took the box again, and took another long, particular look, and give it back to Smiley, and says, very deliberate, "Well, I don't see no p'ints about that frog that's any better'n any other frog."

"May be you don't," Smiley says. "May be you understand frogs, and may be you don't understand 'em; may be you've had experience, and may be you an't only a amature, as it were. Anyways, I've got my opinion, and I'll risk forty dollars that he can outjump any frog in Calaveras county."

And the feller studied a minute, and then says, kinder sad like, "Well, I'm only a stranger here, and I an't got no frog; but if I had a frog, I'd bet you."

And then Smiley says, "That's all right that's all right if you'll hold my box a minute, I'll go and get you a frog." And so the feller took the box, and put up his forty dollars along with Smiley's, and set down to wait.

So he set there a good while thinking and thinking to hisself, and then he got the frog out and **prized** his mouth open and took a tea-spoon and filled him full of quail shot filled him pretty near up to his chin and set him on the floor. Smiley he went to the swamp and slopped around in the mud for a long time, and finally he ketched a frog, and fetched him in, and give him to this feller, and says:

prized – prised, forced open

"Now, if you're ready, set him alongside of Dan'l, with his fore-paws just even with Dan'l, and I'll give the word." Then he says, "One two three jump!" and him and the feller touched up the frogs from behind, and the new frog hopped off, but Dan'l give a heave, and hysted up his shoulders so like a Frenchman, but it wan's no use he couldn't budge; he was planted as solid as an anvil, and he couldn't no more stir than if he was anchored out. Smiley was a good deal surprised, and he was disgusted too, but he didn't have no idea what the matter was, of course.

The feller took the money and started away; and when he was going out at the door, he sorter jerked his thumb over his shoulders this way at Dan'l, and says again, very deliberate, "Well, I don't see no p'ints about that frog that's any better'n any other frog."

Smiley he stood scratching his head and looking down at Dan'l a long time, and at last he says, "I do wonder what in the nation that frog throw'd off for I wonder if there **an't** something the matter with him he 'pears to look mighty baggy, somehow." And he **ketched** Dan'l by the nap of the neck, and lifted him up and says, "Why, blame my cats, if he don't weigh five pound!" and turned him upside down, and he belched out a double handful of shot. And then he see how it was, and he was the maddest man he set the frog down and took out after that feller, but he never ketchd him. And-

an't – isn't

ketched – caught

[Here Simon Wheeler heard his name called from the front yard, and got up to see what was wanted.]

And turning to me as he moved away, he said: "Just set where you are, stranger, and rest easy I an't going to be gone a second."

But, by your leave, I did not think that a continuation of the history of the enterprising **vagabond** Jim Smiley would be likely to afford me much information concerning the Rev. Leonidas W. Smiley, and so I started away.

At the door I met the sociable Wheeler returning, and he **buttonholed** me and recommenced:

"Well, thish-yer Smiley had a **yeller** one-eyed cow that didn't have no tail, only jest a short stump like a bannanner, and..."

"Oh! **hang** Smiley and his **afflicted** cow!" I muttered, good-naturedly, and bidding the old gentleman good-day, I departed.

vagabond – vagrant, tramp

buttonhole – detain in conversation, as if holding on to the outer garments of

yeller – yellow

hang – a mild curse, "the heck with"

afflicted – suffering, distressed

The Celebrated Jumping Frog of Calaveras County

1. The story is set in:
   - A. California
   - B. Colorado
   - C. Missouri

2. The narrator anticipates that the story-teller, Smiley, will be a:
   - A. bore
   - B. liar
   - C. crazy man

3. The characters in the story seem to enjoy:
   - A. gambling
   - B. telling tall tales
   - C. boozing

4. The jumping contest is lost because the title frog is:
   - A. deliberately injured
   - B. overheated
   - C. weighted down

5. The language used in narrating the frog story is best described as:
   - A. local dialect
   - B. jargon
   - C. understated

6. Smiley makes a wager of:
   - A. a steak dinner
   - B. forty dollars
   - C. a bottle of moonshine

7. Smiley says all a frog lacks is:
   - A. flies
   - B. education
   - C. a poke in the rear

8. Smiley holds the jumping contest against:
   - A. Dan'l Webster
   - B. Andrew Jackson
   - C. an unnamed frog

9. At discovering the ruse, Smiley does this to his rival:
   - A. curses a blue streak at him
   - B. grabs him by the nap of the neck
   - C. chases him

10. At a friend's request, the narrator seeks out the Reverend Leonidas W. Smiley, whom the narrator comes to believe is:
    - A. Jim Smiley
    - B. imaginary
    - C. an incurable gambler

Cheshire Cat episode: *Alice in Wonderland*
Lewis Carroll, pen name of Charles Lutwidge Dodgson (1865)

… she was a little startled by seeing the **Cheshire** Cat sitting on a bough of a tree a few yards off.

The Cat only grinned when it saw Alice. It looked good-natured, she thought: still it had *very* long claws and a great many teeth, so she felt that it ought to be treated with respect.

"Cheshire Puss," she began, rather **timidly**, as she did not at all know whether it would like the name: however, it only grinned a little wider. "Come, it's pleased so far," thought Alice, and she went on. "Would you tell me, please, which way I ought to go from here?"

Alice speaks to Cheshire Cat

"That depends a good deal on where you want to get to," said the Cat.

"I don't much care where--" said Alice.

"Then it doesn't matter which way you go," said the Cat.

"--so long as I get *somewhere*," Alice added as an explanation.

"Oh, you're sure to do that," said the Cat, "if you only walk long enough."

Alice felt that this could not be denied, so she tried another question. "What sort of people live about here?"

"In *that* direction," the Cat said, waving its right paw round, "lives a **Hatter**: and in *that* direction," waving the other paw, "lives a March Hare. Visit either you like: they're both **mad**."

"But I don't want to go among mad people," Alice remarked.

Lewis Carroll – writer, mathematician, logician, Anglican deacon, and photographic portraitist

Cheshire – a county in northwest England

timid – lacking confidence, easily frightened, shy

hatter – hat maker/seller

mad – insane, crazy [the mercury used in making fur hats affected hatters' brains]

28

"Oh, you can't help that," said the Cat: "we're all mad here. I'm mad. You're mad."

"How do you know I'm mad?" said Alice.

"You must be," said the Cat, "or you wouldn't have come here."

Alice didn't think that proved it at all; however, she went on "And how do you know that you're mad?"

"To begin with," said the Cat, "a dog's not mad. You grant that?"

"I suppose so," said Alice.

"Well, then," the Cat went on, "you see, a dog growls when it's angry, and wags its tail when it's pleased. Now I growl when I'm pleased, and wag my tail when I'm angry. Therefore I'm mad."

"I call it purring, not growling," said Alice.

"Call it what you like," said the Cat. "Do you play **croquet** with the Queen to-day?"

croquet [krõ-kay´] – a game played on a lawn, in which colored wooden balls are driven through a series of hoops or wickets by means of mallets

"I should like it very much," said Alice, "but I haven't been invited yet."

"You'll see me there," said the Cat, and vanished.

Alice was not much surprised at this, she was getting so used to queer things happening. While she was looking at the place where it had been, it suddenly appeared again.

"By-the-bye, what became of the baby?" said the Cat. "I'd nearly forgotten to ask."

"It turned into a pig," Alice quietly said, just as if it had come back in a natural way.

"I thought it would," said the Cat, and vanished again.

Alice waited a little, half expecting to see it again, but it did not appear, and after a minute or two she walked on in the direction in which the March Hare was said to live. "I've seen hatters before," she said to herself; "the March Hare will be much the most interesting, and perhaps as this is May it won't be raving mad--at least not so mad as it was in March." As she said this, she looked up, and there was the Cat again, sitting on a branch of a tree.

"Did you say pig, or fig?" said the Cat.

"I said pig," replied Alice; "and I wish you wouldn't keep appearing and vanishing so suddenly: you make one quite **giddy**."

giddy – dizzy, overexcited, light-headed

"All right," said the Cat; and this time it vanished quite slowly, beginning with the end of the tail, and ending with the grin, which remained some time after the rest of it had gone.

The Cheshire Cat episode: Alice in Wonderland

1. "Cheshire" here refers to a:
    A. breed of feline
    B. county
    C. kind of cheese

2. The cat is sitting in a:
    A. cradle
    B. basket
    C. tree

3. Alice asks the cat for directions to:
    A. people
    B. the Queen
    C. she doesn't care

4. Alice corrects the cat about the meaning of:
    A. mad
    B. hatter
    C. growl

5. Alice is worried about playing croquet because she:
    A. lacks practice
    B. doesn't know how
    C. has no invitation

6. What is not described as "mad"?
    A. Alice
    B. the cat
    C. a dog

7. The cat says they two will meet in the future at:
    A. the Mad Hatter's
    B. a croquet game
    C. a tea party

8. The cat's vanishing act makes Alice:
    A. cross-eyed
    B. giddy
    C. angry

9. The episode takes place in:
    A. March
    B. April
    C. May

10. Alice treats her conversation with the cat as:
    A. confusing
    B. normal
    C. lacking in reality

A Clean, Well-Lighted Place
Ernest Hemingway (1933)

It was very late and everyone had left the cafe except an old man who sat in the shadow the leaves of the tree made against the electric light. In the day time the street was dusty, but at night the dew settled the dust and the old man liked to sit late because he was deaf and now at night it was quiet and he felt the difference. The two waiters inside the cafe knew that the old man was a little drunk, and while he was a good client they knew that if he became too drunk he would leave without paying, so they kept watch on him.

"Last week he tried to commit suicide," one waiter said.

"Why?"

"He was in despair."

"What about?"

"Nothing."

"How do you know it was nothing?"

"He has plenty of money."

They sat together at a table that was close against the wall near the door of the cafe and looked at the terrace where the tables were all empty except where the old man sat in the shadow of the leaves of the tree that moved slightly in the wind. A girl and a soldier went by in the street. The street light shone on the brass number on his collar. The girl wore no head covering and hurried beside him.

"The guard will pick him up," one waiter said.

"What does it matter if he gets what he's after?"

"He had better get off the street now. The guard will get him. They went by five minutes ago."

Ernest Hemingway – Pulitzer Prize (1953) winner known for his economical and understated prose style

The old man sitting in the shadow rapped on his saucer with his glass. The younger waiter went over to him.

"What do you want?"

The old man looked at him. "Another brandy," he said.

"You'll be drunk," the waiter said. The old man looked at him. The waiter went away.

"He'll stay all night," he said to his colleague. "I'm sleepy now. I never get into bed before three o'clock. He should have killed himself last week."

The waiter took the brandy bottle and another saucer from the counter inside the cafe and marched out to the old man's table. He put down the saucer and poured the glass full of brandy.

"You should have killed yourself last week," he said to the deaf man. The old man motioned with his finger. "A little more," he said. The waiter poured on into the glass so that the brandy slopped over and ran down the stem into the top saucer of the pile. "Thank you," the old man said. The waiter took the bottle back inside the cafe. He sat down at the table with his colleague again.

"He's drunk now," he said.

"He's drunk every night."

"What did he want to kill himself for?"

"How should I know."

"How did he do it?"

"He hung himself with a rope."

"Who cut him down?"

"His niece."

"Why did they do it?"

"Fear for his soul."

"How much money has he got?"

"He's got plenty."

"He must be eighty years old."

"Anyway I should say he was eighty."

"I wish he would go home. I never get to bed before three o'clock. What kind of hour is that to go to bed?"

"He stays up because he likes it."

"He's lonely. I'm not lonely. I have a wife waiting in bed for me."

"He had a wife once too."

"A wife would be no good to him now."

"His niece looks after him."

"I know. You said she cut him down."

"I wouldn't want to be that old. An old man is a nasty thing."

"Not always. This old man is clean. He drinks without spilling. Even now, drunk. Look at him."

"I don't want to look at him. I wish he would go home. He has no regard for those who must work."

The old man looked from his glass across the square, then over at the waiters.

"Another brandy," he said, pointing to his glass. The waiter who was in a hurry came over.

"Finished," he said, speaking with that omission of **syntax** stupid people employ when talking to drunken people or foreigners. "No more tonight. Close now."

syntax – general set of rules for how words and sentences should be structured

"Another," said the old man.

"No. Finished." The waiter wiped the edge of the table with a towel and shook his head.

The old man stood up, slowly counted the saucers, took a leather coin purse from his pocket and paid for the drinks, leaving half a **peseta** tip. The waiter watched him go down the street, a very old man walking unsteadily but with dignity.

peseta – currency of Spain between 1869 and 2002

"Why didn't you let him stay and drink?" the unhurried waiter asked. They were putting up the shutters. "It is not half-past two."

"I want to go home to bed."

"What is an hour?"

"More to me than to him."

"An hour is the same."

"You talk like an old man yourself. He can buy a bottle and drink at home."

"It's not the same."

"No, it is not," agreed the waiter with a wife. He did not wish to be unjust. He was only in a hurry.

"And you? You have no fear of going home before your usual hour?"

"Are you trying to insult me?"

"No, **hombre,** only to make a joke."

hombre – guy, man, fellow (Spanish)

"No," the waiter who was in a hurry said, rising from pulling down the metal shutters. "I have confidence. I am all confidence."

"You have youth, confidence, and a job," the older waiter said. "You have everything."

"And what do you lack?"

"Everything but work."

"You have everything I have."

"No. I have never had confidence and I am not young."

"Come on. Stop talking nonsense and lock up."

"I am of those who like to stay late at the cafe," the older waiter said.

"With all those who do not want to go to bed. With all those who need a light for the night."

"I want to go home and into bed."

"We are of two different kinds," the older waiter said. He was now dressed to go home. "It is not only a question of youth and confidence although those things are very beautiful. Each night I am reluctant to close up because there may be some one who needs the cafe."

"Hombre, there are **bodegas** open all night long."

bodega –
wineshop, barroom

"You do not understand. This is a clean and pleasant cafe. It is well lighted. The light is very good and also, now, there are shadows of the leaves."

"Good night," said the younger waiter.

"Good night," the other said. Turning off the electric light he continued the conversation with himself, It was the light of course but it is necessary that the place be clean and pleasant.

You do not want music. Certainly you do not want music. Nor can you stand before a bar with dignity although that is all that is provided for these hours. What did he fear? It was not a fear or dread, It was a nothing that he knew too well. It was all a nothing and a man was a nothing too. It was only that and light was all it needed and a certain cleanness and order. Some lived in it and never felt it but he knew it all was **nada y pues** nada y nada y pues **nada**. Our nada who art in nada, nada be thy name thy kingdom nada thy will be nada in nada as it is in nada. Give us this nada our daily nada and nada us our nada as we nada our nadas and nada us not into nada but deliver us from nada; pues nada. Hail nothing full of nothing, nothing is with thee. He smiled and stood before a bar with a shining steam pressure coffee machine.

nada y pues – therefore nothing (Sp.)

nada – nothing (Sp.)

"What's yours?" asked the barman.

"Nada."

"**Otro loco mas**," said the barman and turned away.

otro loco mas – another crazy person (Sp.)

"A little cup," said the waiter.

The barman poured it for him.

"The light is very bright and pleasant but the bar is unpolished," the waiter said.

The barman looked at him but did not answer. It was too late at night for conversation.

"You want another **copita**?" the barman asked.

copita – glass of sherry (Sp.)

"No, thank you," said the waiter and went out. He disliked bars and bodegas. A clean, well-lighted cafe was a very different thing. Now, without thinking further, he would go home to his room. He would lie in the bed and finally, with daylight, he would go to sleep. After all, he said to himself, it's probably only insomnia. Many must have it.

37

A Clean Well-Lighted Place

1. The story takes place in:
   A. Mexico
   B. New Mexico
   C. Spain

2. A "bodega" is best described as a:
   A. small hotel
   B. saloon
   C. restaurant

3. The prevailing mood of the old man is:
   A. despair
   B. panic
   C. caution

4. The old man is said to have attempted suicide in despair over:
   A. his daughter
   B. money
   C. nothing

5. The older waiter's attitude in general can be described as:
   A. cynical
   B. sympathetic
   C. caring

6. The waiter repeats the word "nada" (p.37) mixed with the words of a:
   A. poem
   B. prayer
   C. song

7. The word "nada" repeatedly used by the older waiter indicates:
   A. intoxication
   B. craziness
   C. futility

8. The story is mostly told:
   A. by the older waiter
   B. by the bartender
   C. through dialogue

9. The old man was saved from hanging by:
   A. prayer
   B. his niece
   C. the barman

10. The atmosphere of the external situation is suggested as:
    A. militaristic
    B. romantic
    C. sunny

The Code of Hammurabi – Excerpt
1780 BCE

When **Marduk** sent me, Hammurabi, to rule over men, to give the protection of right to the land, I did right and righteousness in ..., and brought about the well-being of the oppressed.

Code of Laws

1. If anyone ensnare another, putting a ban upon him, but he cannot prove it, then he that ensnared him shall be put to death.

2. If anyone bring an accusation against a man, and the accused go to the river and leap into the river, if he sink in the river his accuser shall take possession of his house. But if the river prove that the accused is not guilty, and he escape unhurt, then he who had brought the accusation shall be put to death, while he who leaped into the river shall take possession of the house that had belonged to his accuser.

3. If anyone bring an accusation of any crime before the elders, and does not prove what he has charged, he shall, if it be a **capital** offense charged, be put to death.

4. If he satisfy the elders to impose a fine of grain or money, he shall receive the fine that the action produces.

5. If a judge try a case, reach a decision, and present his judgment in writing; if later error shall appear in his decision, and it be through his own fault, then he shall pay twelve times the fine set by him in the case, and he shall be publicly removed from the judge's bench, and never again shall he sit there to render judgment.

6. If anyone steal the property of a temple or of the court, he shall be put to death, and also the one who receives the stolen thing from him shall be put to death.

7. If anyone buy from the son or the slave of another man, without witnesses or a contract, silver or gold, a male or

Hammurabi – first king of the **Babylonian** Empire and originator of one of the first written codes of law

Babylonia – modern day southern Iraq

Marduk – chief deity of the Babylonians

capital – punishable by death

female slave, an ox or a sheep, an ass or anything, or if he take it in charge, he is considered a thief and shall be put to death.

8. If anyone steal cattle or sheep, or an ass, or a pig or a goat, if it belong to a god or to the court, the thief shall pay thirty-fold therefor; if they belonged to a freed man of the king he shall pay tenfold; if the thief has nothing with which to pay he shall be put to death.

9. If anyone lose an article, and find it in the possession of another: if the person in whose possession the thing is found say "A merchant sold it to me, I paid for it before witnesses," and if the owner of the thing say, "I will bring witnesses who know my property," then shall the purchaser bring the merchant who sold it to him, and the witnesses before whom he bought it, and the owner shall bring witnesses who can identify his property. The judge shall examine their testimony--both of the witnesses before whom the price was paid, and of the witnesses who identify the lost article on oath. The merchant is then proved to be a thief and shall be put to death. The owner of the lost article receives his property, and he who bought it receives the money he paid from the estate of the merchant.

10. If the purchaser does not bring the merchant and the witnesses before whom he bought the article, but its owner bring witnesses who identify it, then the buyer is the thief and shall be put to death, and the owner receives the lost article.

11. If the owner does not bring witnesses to identify the lost article, he is an evil-doer, he has **traduced**, and shall be put to death.

traduced – slandered, defamed, spoken ill of

12. If the witnesses be not at hand, then shall the judge set a limit, at the expiration of six months. If his witnesses have not appeared within the six months, he is an evil-doer, and shall bear the fine of the pending case.

[Editor's note: there is no 13th law in the code, 13 being considered an unlucky and evil number]

14. If anyone steal the minor son of another, he shall be put to death.

15. If anyone take a male or female slave of the court, or a male or female slave of a freed man, outside the city gates, he shall be put to death.

major domus – chief steward in a grand household, especially of a sovereign

16. If anyone receive into his house a runaway male or female slave of the court, or of a freedman, and does not bring it out at the public proclamation of the **major domus**, the master of the house shall be put to death.

The Code of Hammurabi

1. Hammurabi was the name of a:
   A. tribe
   B. judge
   C. ruler

2. A "code" here means a set of:
   A. rituals
   B. secret writings
   C. laws

3. If a defendant drowns in a trial by water, his property will go to the:
   A. accuser
   B. treasury
   C. king

4. The code's numbered list of provisions shows the Babylonians were:
   A. logical
   B. superstitious
   C. litigious

5. A judge who renders a faulty decision is:
   A. put to death
   B. removed from office
   C. publicly flogged

6. Hammurabi himself claims to have been sent by Marduk and subsequently served:
   A. the oppressed
   B. the law
   C. protection from enemies

7. A man failing a trial by water (law #2) would seem to be:
   A. granted his accuser's house
   B. accursed before the law
   C. dead

8. The major domus is one who:
   A. a master of the house
   B. represents the king
   C. heads the household

9. A thief of livestock from a god who cannot pay the prescribed judgment is penalized by:
   A. future payment of tenfold
   B. life imprisonment
   C. death

10. There is no recorded 13th law because:
   A. there are only 12 members of a jury
   B. 13 is considered evil
   C. only the first 12 enumerated offenses are capital crimes

The Death of Socrates: Plato's Phaedo
399 BCE

Socrates' death at 70 was the result of his asking philosophical questions. A majority of the Athenian citizens chosen by lot as jurors voted to convict him of corrupting the youth. He was taken to the nearby jail where his sentence would be carried out. Athenian law prescribed death by drinking a cup of poison **hemlock**. Socrates would be his own executioner.

Then he turned to us, and added with a smile: "I cannot make **Crito** believe that I am the same Socrates who has been talking and conducting the argument; he **fancies** that I am the other Socrates whom he will soon see, a dead body--and he asks, How shall he bury me? And though I have spoken many words in the endeavor to show that when I have drunk the poison I shall leave you and go to the joys of the blessed-- these words of mine, with which I was comforting you and myself, have had, as I perceive, no effect upon Crito. And therefore I want you to be **surety** for me to him how, as at the trial he was surety to the judges for me: but let the promise be of another sort; for he was surety for me to the judges that I would remain, and you must be my surety to him that I shall not remain, but go away and depart; and then he will suffer less at my death, and not be grieved when he sees my body being burned or buried. I would not have him sorrow at my hard **lot**, or say at the burial, Thus we lay out Socrates, or Thus we follow him to the grave or bury him; for false words are not only evil in themselves, but they infect the soul with evil. Be of good cheer then, my dear Crito, and say that you are burying my body only, and do with that whatever is usual, and what you think best."

When he had spoken these words, he arose and went into a chamber to bathe; Crito followed him and told us to wait. So we remained behind, talking and thinking of the subject of **discourse**, and also of the greatness of our sorrow; he was like a father of whom we were being **bereaved**, and we were about to pass the rest of our lives as orphans. When he had taken the bath his children were brought to him (he had two young sons and an elder one); and the women of his family also came, and he talked to them and gave them a few

Socrates – Greek philosopher whose method of Q. and A. is captured in the dialogues of Plato, his greatest pupil

hemlock – poisonous plant of the parsley family

Crito – Socrates refused this friend's offer to finance a prison escape

fancies – imagines

surety – guarantee

lot – fate, fortune

discourse – conversation

bereaved – sad at the death of a loved one

directions in the presence of Crito; then he dismissed them and returned to us.

Now the hour of sunset was near, for a good deal of time had passed while he was within. When he came out, he sat down with us again after his bath, but not much was said. Soon the jailer, who was the servant of the eleven, entered and stood by him, saying: "To you, Socrates, whom I know to be the noblest and gentlest and best of all who ever came to this place, I will not **impute** the angry feelings of other men, who rage and swear at me, when, in obedience to the authorities, I bid them drink the poison--indeed, I am sure that you will not be angry with me; for others, as you are aware, and not I, are to blame. And so fare you well, and try to bear lightly what must needs be--you know my errand." Then bursting into tears he turned away and went out.

impute – ascribe, assign blame or responsibility

Socrates looked at him and said: "I return your good wishes, and will do as you bid." Then turning to us, he said, "How charming the man is: since I have been in prison he has always been coming to see me, and at times he would talk to me, and was as good to me as could be, and now see how generously he sorrows on my account. We must do as he says, Crito; and therefore let the cup be brought, if the poison is prepared; if not, let the attendant prepare some."

"Yet," said Crito, "the sun is still upon the hilltops, and I know that many a one has taken the **draught** late, and after the announcement has been made to him, he has eaten and drunk, and enjoyed the society of his beloved; do not hurry--there is time enough."

draught – a portion of liquid to be drunk, especially of medicine

Socrates said: "Yes, Crito, and they of whom you speak are right in so acting, for they think that they will be gainers by the delay; But I am right in not following their example, for I do not think that I should gain anything by drinking the poison a little later; I should only be ridiculous in my own eyes for sparing and saving a life which is already **forfeit**. Please then to do as I say, and not to refuse me."

forfeit – lost or surrendered as punishment

Crito made a sign to the servant, who was standing by; and he went out, and having been absent for some time, returned

with the jailer carrying the cup of poison. Socrates said:
"You, my good friend, who are experienced in these matters,
shall give me directions how I am to proceed."

The man answered: "you have only to walk about until your
legs are heavy, and then to lie down, and the poison will act."

At the same time he handed the cup to Socrates, who in the
easiest and gentlest manner, without the least fear or change
of color or feature, looking at the man with all his eyes, . . . as
his manner was, took the cup and said: "What do you say
about making a **libation** out of this cup to any god? May I, or
not?"

The man answered: "We only prepare, Socrates, just so much
as we deem enough."

"I understand," he said; "but I may and must ask the gods to
prosper my journey from this to the other world--even so--
and so be it according to my prayer.

Then raising the cup to his lips, quite readily and cheerfully
he drank off the poison. And hitherto most of us had been
able to control our sorrow; but now when we saw him
drinking, and saw too that he had finished the draught, we
could not longer **forbear**, and in spite of myself my own tears
were flowing fast; so that I covered my face and wept, not for
him, but at the thought of my own **calamity** in having to part
from such a friend. Nor was I the first; for Crito, when he
found himself unable to restrain his tears, had got up, and I
followed; and at that moment, Apollodorus, who had been
weeping all the time, broke out in a loud and passionate cry
which made cowards of us all.

Socrates alone retained his calmness: "What is this strange
outcry?" he said. "I sent away the women mainly in order that
they might not misbehave in this way, for I have been told
that a man should die in peace. Be quiet then, and have
patience."

When we heard his words we were ashamed, and refrained
our tears; and he walked about until, as he said, his legs began

to fail, and then he lay on his back, according to the directions, and the man who gave him the poison now and then looked at his feet and legs; and after a while he pressed his foot hard, and asked him if he could feel; and he said, "No;" and then his leg, and so upwards and upwards, and showed us that he was cold and stiff. And he felt them himself, and said: "When the poison reaches the heart, that will be the end."

He was beginning to grow cold about the groin, when he uncovered his face, for he had covered himself up, and said-- they were his last words--he said: "Crito, I owe a **cock** to Asclepius; will you remember to pay the debt?

cock – rooster, adult male chicken

"The debt shall be paid," said Crito; "is there anything else?"

There was no answer to this question; but in a minute or two a movement was heard, and the attendants uncovered him; his eyes were set, and Crito closed his eyes and mouth.

Such was the end . . . of our friend; concerning whom I may truly say, that of all the men of his time whom I have known, he was the wisest and justest and best.

The Death of Socrates

1. Socrates was condemned for this crime:
    A. blasphemy
    B. questioning authority
    C. corrupting the young

2. The Socratic Method deals with:
    A. civil punishment
    B. teaching
    C. experimentation

3. The hemlock mentioned here is a kind of poisonous:
    A. pine
    B. wildflower
    C. parsley

4. Crito is Socrates':
    A. accuser
    B. jailer
    C. friend

5. Socrates is advised that to hasten death after drinking the hemlock, he should:
    A. pray
    B. walk
    C. immerse himself in the baths

6. The last to speak to Socrates is:
    A. the jailer
    B. Socrates' wife
    C. Crito

7. Socrates' death is said to make these people "pass the rest of (their) lives as orphans":
    A. his followers
    B. his sons
    C. the citizen of Athens

8. The jailer's final words indicate he himself feels:
    A. blameless
    B. generous
    C. evil

9. Socrates says that by delaying drinking the poison he would be:
    A. ridiculous
    B. avoiding the inevitable
    C. dishonorable

10. Socrates' final remark relates to:
    A. paying a debt
    B. sending his wife away
    C. saying farewell to Crito

The Death of the Moth
Virginia Woolf 1941

Moths that fly by day are not properly to be called moths; they do not excite that pleasant sense of dark autumn nights and ivy-blossom which the commonest **yellow-underwing** asleep in the shadow of the curtain never fails to rouse in us.

They are hybrid creatures, neither gay like butterflies nor somber like their own species. Nevertheless the present specimen, with his narrow hay-colored wings, fringed with a tassel of the same color, seemed to be content with life. It was a pleasant morning, mid-September, mild, **benignant**, yet with a keener breath than that of the summer months. The plough was already **scoring** the field opposite the window, and where the **share** had been, the earth was pressed flat and gleamed with moisture. Such vigor came rolling in from the fields and the down beyond that it was difficult to keep the eyes strictly turned upon the book. The **rooks** too were keeping one of their annual festivities; soaring round the tree tops until it looked as if a vast net with thousands of black knots in it had been cast up into the air; which, after a few moments sank slowly down upon the trees until every twig seemed to have a knot at the end of it. Then, suddenly, the net would be thrown into the air again in a wider circle this time, with the utmost clamor and **vociferation**, as though to be thrown into the air and settle slowly down upon the tree tops were a tremendously exciting experience.

The same energy which inspired the rooks, the ploughmen, the horses, and even, it seemed, the lean bare-backed **downs**, sent the moth fluttering from side to side of his square of the windowpane. One could not help watching him. One, was, indeed, conscious of a queer feeling of pity for him. The possibilities of pleasure seemed that morning so enormous and so various that to have only a moth's part in life, and a day moth's at that, appeared a hard fate, and his zest in enjoying his meager opportunities to the full, pathetic. He flew vigorously to one corner of his compartment, and, after waiting there a second, flew across to the other. What remained for him but to fly to a third corner and then to a fourth? That was all he could do, in spite of the size of the

Virginia Woolf – British modernist author and early feminist who drowned herself at news of the onset of World War II

yellow underwing – species of large moth

benignant – serenely mild, favorable, benign

scoring – scratching or incising with a sharp instrument

share – the horizontal cutting blade of a plow

rooks – crows

vociferation – noisy outcry

downs – low, grassy hills

48

downs, the width of the sky, the far-off smoke of houses, and the romantic voice, now and then, of a steamer thin but pure, of the enormous energy of the world had been thrust into his frail and **diminutive** body. As often as he crossed the pane, I could **fancy** that a thread of vital light became visible. He was little or nothing but life.

Yet, because he was so small, and so simple a form of the energy that was rolling in at the open window and driving its way through so many narrow and intricate corridors in my own brain and in those of other human beings, there was something marvelous as well as pathetic about him. It was as if someone had taken a tiny bead of pure life and **decking** it as lightly as possible with down and feathers, had set it dancing and zigzagging to show us the true nature of life. Thus displayed one could not get over the strangeness of it. One is **apt** to forget all about life, seeing it humped and **bossed** and garnished and **cumbered** so that it has to move with the greatest **circumspection** and dignity. Again, the thought of all that life might have been had he been born in any other shape caused one to view his simple activities with a kind of pity.

After a time, tired by his dancing apparently, he settled on the window ledge in the sun, and, the queer spectacle being at an end, I forgot about him. Then, looking up, my eye was caught by him. He was trying to resume his dancing, but seemed either so stiff or so awkward that he could only flutter to the bottom of the windowpane; and when he tried to fly across it he failed. Being **intent** on other matters I watched these futile attempts for a time without thinking, unconsciously waiting for him to resume his flight, as one waits for a machine, that has stopped momentarily, to start again without considering the reason of its failure. After perhaps a seventh attempt he slipped from the wooden ledge and fell, fluttering his wings, on to his back on the windowsill. The helplessness of his attitude roused me. It flashed upon me that he was in difficulties; he could no longer raise himself; his legs struggled vainly. But, as I stretched out a pencil, meaning to help him to right himself, it came over me that the failure and

diminutive – extremely or unusually small

fancy – imagine

decking – decorating

apt – likely

bossed – ornamented

cumbered – hampered

circumspection – being wary, prudent, unwilling to take risks, cautious

intent – preoccupied, attending to, absorbed with

awkwardness were the approach of death. I laid the pencil down again.

The legs **agitated** themselves once more. I looked as if for the enemy against which he struggled. I looked out of doors. What had happened there? Presumably it was midday, and work in the fields had stopped. Stillness and quiet had replaced the previous animation. The birds had taken themselves off to feed in the brooks. The horses stood still. Yet the power was there all the same, massed outside, indifferent, impersonal, not attending to anything in particular. Somehow it was opposed to the little hay-colored moth. It was useless to try to do anything. One could only watch the extraordinary efforts made by those tiny legs against an oncoming doom which could, had it chosen, have submerged an entire city, not merely a city, but masses of human beings; nothing, I knew, had any chance against death. Nevertheless after a pause of exhaustion the legs fluttered again. It was superb this last protest, and so frantic that he succeeded at last in righting himself. One's sympathies, of course, were all on the side of life. Also, when there was nobody to care or to know, this gigantic effort on the part of an insignificant little moth, against a power of such magnitude, to retain what no one else valued or desired to keep, moved one strangely. Again, somehow, one saw life, a pure bead. I lifted the pencil again, useless though I knew it to be. But even as I did so, the unmistakable tokens of death showed themselves. The body relaxed, and instantly grew stiff. The struggle was over. The insignificant little creature now knew death. As I looked at the dead moth, this **minute** wayside triumph of so great a force over so mean an antagonist filled me with wonder. Just as life had been strange a few minutes before, so death was now as strange. The moth having righted himself now lay most decently and uncomplainingly composed. O yes, he seemed to say, death is stronger than I am.

agitated – move in violent or irregular action

minute [mī-nōōt′] – tiny

The Death of the Moth

1. Moths are said here to be differentiated from butterflies by:
    A. when they fly
    B. coloration
    C. clustering behavior

2. The time of year described is:
    A. early spring
    B. mid-summer
    C. fall

3. The natural world distracts the author from her:
    A. knitting
    B. writing
    C. reading

4. The "vast net with 1000s of black knots" refers to the movement of:
    A. crows
    B. insects
    C. fishing boats

5. The author is sitting:
    A. on a grassy meadow
    B. in a house
    C. under a tree

6. The author first sees the moth as an emblem of:
    A. nature's variety
    B. pure life
    C. uncontrolled energy

7. The "compartment" whose corners the moth explores is:
    A. a window pane
    B. a bird feeder
    C. a ledge

8. The pencil is used in an attempt to:
    A. tease the moth
    B. study the moth closely
    C. help the moth

9. The moth, struggling on its back, is finally righted by:
    A. its own efforts
    B. a puff of wind
    C. the narrator

10. At the end, the moth seems to the author:
    A. boastful
    B. defiant
    C. resigned

The Destiny of Colored Americans
Frederick Douglass 1849

It is impossible to settle, by the light of the present, and by the experience of the past, any thing, definitely and absolutely, as to the future condition of the colored people of this country; but, so far as present indications determine, it is clear that this land must continue to be the home of the colored man so long as it remains the **abode** of civilization and religion. For more than two hundred years we have been identified with its soil, its products, and its institutions; under the sternest and bitterest circumstances of slavery and oppression--under the lash of Slavery at the South--under the sting of prejudice and **malice** at the North--and under hardships the most unfavorable to existence and population, we have lived, and continue to live and **increase**. The persecuted red man of the forest, the original owner of the soil, has, step by step, retreated from the Atlantic lakes and rivers; escaping, as it were, before the footsteps of the white man, and gradually disappearing from the face of the country. He looks upon the steamboats, the railroads, and canals, cutting and crossing his former hunting grounds; and upon the ploughshare, throwing up the bones of his **venerable** ancestors, and beholds his glory departing--and his heart sickens at the desolation. He spurns the civilization--he hates the race which has **despoiled** him, and unable to measure arms with his superior foe, he dies. Not so with the black man. More unlike the European in form, feature and color-- called to endure greater hardships, injuries and insults than those to which the Indians have been subjected, he yet lives and prospers under every disadvantage. Long have his enemies sought to **expatriate** him, and to teach his children that this is not their home, but in spite of all their cunning schemes, and subtle **contrivances**, his footprints yet mark the soil of his birth, and he gives every indication that America will, forever, remain the home of his **posterity**. We deem it a settled point that the destiny of the colored man is bound up with that of the white people of his country; be the destiny of the latter what it may.

Frederick Douglass – former slave and eminent human rights leader in the abolition movement as orator and writer

abode – dwelling place, home, residence

malice – desire to cause harm to another person, ill will

increase – reproduce, grow in population

venerable – respected because of age, wisdom, or character

despoiled – deprived, plundered

expatriate – banishment, expulsion from a native country

contrivance – clever plan or trick

posterity – one's offspring, future generations

It is **idle**--worse than idle, ever to think of our expatriation, or removal. The history of the colonization society must extinguish all such **speculations**. We are rapidly filling up the number of four millions; and all the gold of California combined, would be insufficient to **defray** the expenses attending our colonization. We are, as laborers, too essential to the interests of our white fellow-countrymen, to make a very grand effort to drive us from this country among probable events. While labor is needed, the laborer cannot fail to be valued; and although passion and prejudice may sometimes **vociferate** against us, and demand our expulsion, such efforts will only be **spasmodic**, and can never prevail against the sober second thought of self-interest. *We are here*, and here we are likely to be. To imagine that we shall ever be eradicated is absurd and ridiculous. We can be remodified, changed, and assimilated, but never extinguished. We repeat, therefore, that *we are here*; and that this is *our* country; and the question for the philosophers and statesmen of the land ought to be, What principles should dictate the policy of the action towards us? We shall neither die out, nor be driven out; but shall go with this people, either as a testimony against them, or as an evidence in their favor throughout their generations. We are clearly on their hands, and must remain there forever. All this we say for the benefit of those who hate the Negro more than they love their country. In an article, under the caption of "Government and its Subjects" (published in our last week's paper), we called attention to the unwise, as well as the unjust policy usually adopted, by our Government, towards its colored citizens. We would continue to direct our attention to that policy, and in our humble way, we would **remonstrate** against it, as fraught with evil to the white man, as well as to his victim.

The white man's happiness cannot be **purchased** by the black man's misery. Virtue cannot prevail among the white people, by its destruction among the black people, who form a part of the whole community. It is evident that the white and black "must fall or flourish together." In the light of this great truth, laws ought to be enacted, and institutions established--all distinctions, founded on complexion, ought to be repealed, repudiated, and forever abolished--and every right, privilege,

idle – vain, pointless, without purpose

speculation – surmise or conjecture

defray – pay for

vociferate – speak loudly, bellow

spasmodic – fitful, intermittent

remonstrate – give reasons against, complain to an authority

purchase – acquire, obtain, gain

and immunity, now enjoyed by the white man, ought to be as freely granted to the man of color.

Where "knowledge is power," that nation is the most powerful which has the largest population of intelligent men; for a nation to cramp, and **circumscribe** the mental faculties of a class of its inhabitants, is as unwise as it is cruel, since it, in the same proportion, sacrifices its power and happiness. The American people, in the light of this reasoning, are at this moment, in obedience to their pride and folly (we say nothing of the wickedness of the act), wasting one-sixth part of the energies of the entire nation by transforming three millions of its men into beasts of burden. What a loss to industry, skill, invention (to say nothing of its foul and corrupting influence) is *Slavery*! How it ties the hand, cramps the mind, darkens the understanding, and paralyses the whole man! Nothing is more evident to a man who reasons at all, than that America is acting an irrational part in continuing the slave system at the South, and in oppressing its free colored citizens at the North. Regarding the nation as an individual, the act of enslaving and oppressing thus, is as wild and senseless as it would be for **Nicholas** to order the amputation of the right arm of every Russian soldier before engaging in war with France. We again repeat that Slavery is the peculiar weakness of America, as well as its peculiar crime; and the day may yet come with this visionary and oft repeated declaration will be found to contain a great truth.

circumscribe – restrict, limit

Nicholas – czar of Russia at the time

The Destiny of Colored Americans

1. Unlike Negroes, native Americans are said to have reacted to oppression by:
   A. armed resistance
   B. open protest
   C. retreating

2. Douglass says it is pointless to think of Negroes ending up:
   A. uprooted from the land
   B. assimilated
   C. disloyal

3. Douglass condemns the South for slavery of the Negroes, while the North is faulted for:
   A. prejudice
   B. isolation of colored people
   C. unfair laws

4. Douglass claims what makes a powerful country is:
   A. equal citizens
   B. intelligent men
   C. free men

5. Douglass declares it "unwise" to "cramp" the Negroes':
   A. minds
   B. social mobility
   C. freedom

6. The word "expatriate" as used here (¶ 1) most nearly means:
   A. deprive of citizenship
   B. expel
   C. disown

7. Douglass writes that "the white man's happiness" cannot be attained by the black man's:
   A. enslavement
   B. labor
   C. misery

8. Based on its content, this passage was written:
   A. before the Civil War
   B. during the Civil War
   C. before the Emancipation Proclamation

9. Douglass claims that "all the gold of California" could not pay for slaves':
   A. past suffering
   B. past service
   C. relocation

10. In the final paragraph, Czar Nicholas is invoked to stress that continued enslavement:
    A. is irrational
    B. weakens national defenses
    C. breeds rebellion

The Diary of Anne Frank Excerpts 1942-1944

Anne Frank was a 14-year-old German Jew in hiding from the Nazis in the attic of a Netherlands house during World War II.

On Deportations

"Our many Jewish friends and acquaintances are being taken away in **droves**. The **Gestapo** is treating them very roughly and transporting them in **cattle cars** to Westerbork, the big camp in Drenthe to which they're sending all the Jews....If it's that bad in Holland, what must it be like in those faraway and uncivilized places where the Germans are sending them? We assume that most of them are being murdered. The English radio says they're being gassed." – *October 9, 1942*

On Nazi Punishment of Resisters

"Have you ever heard the term '**hostages**'? That's the latest punishment for **saboteurs**. It's the most horrible thing you can imagine. Leading citizens - innocent people - are taken prisoner to await their execution. If the Gestapo can't find the saboteur, they simply grab five hostages and line them up against the wall. You read the announcements of their death in the paper, where they're referred to as 'fatal accidents'."
– *October 9, 1942*

"All college students are being asked to sign an official statement to the effect that they 'sympathize with the Germans and approve of the New Order.' Eighty percent have decided to obey the **dictates** of their conscience, but the penalty will be severe. Any student refusing to sign will be sent to a German labor camp." – *May 18, 1943*

On Writing and Her Diary

"Mr. Bolkenstein, the Cabinet Minister, speaking on the Dutch broadcast from London, said that after the war a collection would be made of diaries and letters dealing with the war. Of course, everyone pounced on my diary."
– *March 29, 1944*

---

deportation – throwing or transporting a foreigner out of a country

droves – large crowd or herd

Gestapo – Nazi official secret police

cattle cars – railroad freight cars, especially to transport livestock

hostage – someone taken prisoner in order to enforce the taker's demands

saboteur – person who deliberately destroys or obstructs for political or military advantage

dictate – ruling or guiding principle

"When I write, I can shake off all my cares." – *April 5, 1944*

Describing Her Despair

"I've reached the point where I hardly care whether I live or die. The world will keep on turning without me, and I can't do anything to change events anyway. I'll just let matters take their course and concentrate on studying and hope that everything will be all right in the end." – *February 3, 1944*

"...but the minute I was alone I knew I was going to cry my eyes out. I slid to the floor in my nightgown and began by saying my prayers, very **fervently**. Then I drew my knees to my chest, lay my head on my arms and cried, all huddled up on the bare floor. A loud sob brought me back down to earth..." – *April 5, 1944*

fervent – exhibiting great intensity of feeling; zealous

On Her Old Country, Germany

"Fine specimens of humanity, those Germans, and to think I'm actually one of them! No, that's not true, Hitler took away our nationality long ago. And besides, there are no greater enemies on earth than the Germans and Jews."
– *October 9, 1942*

On Still Believing

"It's a wonder I haven't abandoned all my ideals, they seem so absurd and impractical. Yet I cling to them because I still believe, in spite of everything, that people are truly good at heart. It's utterly impossible for me to build my life on a foundation of chaos, suffering, and death. I see the world being slowly transformed into a wilderness, I hear the approaching thunder that, one day, will destroy us too, I feel the suffering of millions. And yet, when I look up at the sky, I somehow feel that everything will change for the better, that this cruelty too shall end, that peace and **tranquility** will return once more." – *July 15, 1944*

tranquil – calm, free of commotion, peaceful

Bergen-Belsen – a Nazi concentration camp in Northern Germany

In March of 1945, nine months after she was arrested, Anne Frank died of typhus at **Bergen-Belsen**. She was fifteen years old.

The Diary of Anne Frank

1. Anne Frank's nationality is:
   A. Dutch
   B. German
   C. Austrian

2. Germans' greatest enemies are said to be the:
   A. Allies
   B. English
   C. Jews

3. When Anne calls her countrymen "fine specimens of humanity", she is being:
   A. humorous
   B. sarcastic
   C. proud

4. To take her mind off her troubles, Anne retreats to:
   A. her bed
   B. studies
   C. daydreaming

5. Those around her express interest in Anne's:
   A. diary
   B. escape
   C. future

6. The English language radio station reports that the Jews are being:
   A. deported
   B. gassed
   C. executed

7. Those 80% of students refusing to sign a document saying they sympathize with the Germans' "New Order" are:
   A. denied further studies
   B. publicly humiliated
   C. sent to labor camps

8. After a London broadcast, "everyone pounced on" Anne Frank because of her:
   A. disloyalty
   B. diary
   C. Jewish heritage

9. Anne writes that these "seem so absurd and impractical":
   A. her dreams
   B. her hopes for survival
   C. her ideals

10. In Anne's final diary entry, her attitude is one of:
   A. optimism
   B. dread
   C. forgiveness

The Discovery of Radium

Marie Curie – speech at Vassar College in Poughkeepsie, N.Y., May 14, 1921

I could tell you many things about **radium** and **radioactivity** and it would take a long time. But as we cannot do that, I shall only give you a short account of my early work about radium. Radium is no more a baby, it is more than twenty years old, but the conditions of the discovery were somewhat peculiar, and so it is always of interest to remember them and to explain them.

We must go back to the year 1897. **Professor Curie** and I worked at that time in the laboratory of the school of Physics and Chemistry where Professor Curie held his lectures. I was engaged in some work on uranium rays which had been discovered two years before by **Professor Becquerel**.

I spent some time in studying the way of making good measurements of the uranium rays, and then I wanted to know if there were other elements, giving out rays of the same kind. So I took up a work about all known elements, and their compounds and found that uranium compounds are active and also all **thorium** compounds, but other elements were not found active, nor were their compounds. As for the uranium and thorium compounds, I found that they were active in proportion to their uranium or thorium content. The more uranium or thorium, the greater the activity, the activity being an atomic property of the elements, uranium and thorium.

Them I took up measurements of minerals and I found that several of those which contain uranium or thorium or both were active. But then the activity was not what I could expect, it was greater than for uranium or thorium compounds like the oxides which are almost entirely composed of these elements.

Then I thought that there should be in the minerals some unknown element having a much greater radioactivity than uranium or thorium. And I wanted to find and to separate that element, and I settled to that work with Professor Curie. We

Marie Curie – Polish born, naturalized French scientist; first woman Nobel prize winner

radium – element discovered in 1898 by Marie and Pierre Curie

radioactivity – spontaneous emission of radiation, either directly from unstable atomic nuclei or as a consequence of a nuclear reaction

Pierre Curie – French physicist and 1903 Nobel Prize winner with his wife, Marie, and Henri Becquerel

Henri Becquerel – Nobel prize-winning discoverer of radioactivity for whom its measure is named

thorium – radioactive metallic element – one of whose forms (isotopes) has a half-life of 14 billion years

thought it would be done in several weeks or months, but it was not so. It took many years of hard work to finish that task. There was not one new element, there were several of them. But the most important is radium, which could be separated in a pure state.

Now, the special interest of radium is in the intensity of its rays which several million times greater than the uranium rays. And the effects of the rays make the radium so important. If we take a practical point of view, then the most important property of the rays is the production of **physiological** effects on the cells of the human organism. These effects may be used for the cure of several diseases. Good results have been obtained in many cases. What is considered particularly important is the treatment of cancer. The medical utilization of radium makes it necessary to get that element in sufficient quantities. And so a factory of radium was started to begin with in France, and later in America where a big quantity of ore named carnotite is available. America does produce many **grams** of radium every year, but the price is still very high because the quantity of radium contained in the ore is so small. The radium is more than a hundred thousand times **dearer** than gold.

But we must not forget that when radium was discovered no one knew that it would prove useful in hospitals. The work was one of pure science. And this is a proof that scientific work must not be considered from the point of view of the direct usefulness of it. It must be done for itself, for the beauty of science, and then there is always the chance that a scientific discovery may become like the radium a benefit for humanity.

The scientific history of radium is beautiful. The properties of the rays have been studied very closely. We know that particles are expelled from radium with a very great velocity near to that of the light. We know that the atoms of radium are destroyed by expulsion of these particles, some of which are atoms of helium. And in that way it has been proved that the radioactive elements are constantly disintegrating and that they produce at the end ordinary elements, principally helium and lead. That is, as you see, a theory of transformation of

physiological – relating to normal functioning of a living organism

gram – metric system unit of mass equal to one small paper clip

dearer – costlier, more expensive

atoms which are not stable, as was believed before, but may undergo spontaneous changes.

Radium is not alone in having these properties. Many having other radio-elements are known already, the polonium, the mesothorium, the radiothorium, the actinium. We know also radioactive gases, named emanations. There is a great variety of substances and effects in radioactivity. There is always a vast field left to experimentation and I hope that we may have some beautiful progress in the following years. It is my earnest desire that some of you should carry on this scientific work and keep for your ambition the determination to make a permanent contribution to science.

Discovery of Radium

1. Marie Curie was a naturalized citizen of:
   - A. France
   - B. Poland
   - C. the U.S.

2. Curie is addressing:
   - A. fellow physicists
   - B. government researchers
   - C. college students

3. The effort to separate and isolate radium took several:
   - A. years
   - B. months
   - C. days

4. Curie found radioactivity's "most important property" to be those rays use in:
   - A. armaments
   - B. treating disease
   - C. chain reactions

5. Radium is said over time to decay into:
   - A. hydrogen
   - B. lead
   - C. plutonium

6. The word "*physiological*" as used here (¶ 6) most nearly relates to:
   - A. the body
   - B. laws of physics
   - C. the brain

7. Curie notes that compared to gold, radium is over a hundred thousand times more:
   - A. atomically active
   - B. rare
   - C. expensive

8. Curie reports that radium was found to be useful in:
   - A. clock faces
   - B. hospitals
   - C. lights

9. Curie's initial work with radium was in the interest of:
   - A. pure science
   - B. its chemical applications
   - C. its human benefits

10. Curie's experiments with radioactivity began:
   - A. the end of the 19th century
   - B. in the 1920s
   - C. in secrecy

Eisenhower's Farewell Address – 1961

The Supreme Allied Commander in WWII and later U.S. President Dwight D. Eisenhower, in this final speech warned against the potential influence of what he called the "military-industrial complex".

My fellow Americans:

… We now stand ten years past the midpoint of a century that has witnessed four major wars among great nations…

A vital element in keeping the peace is our military establishment. Our arms must be mighty, ready for instant action, so that no potential aggressor may be tempted to risk his own destruction.

Our military organization today bears little relation to that known by any of my predecessors in peacetime, or indeed by the fighting men of World War II or **Korea**.

Korea – the Korean War occurred 1950-1953

Until the latest of our world conflicts, the United States had no **armaments** industry. American makers of **plowshares** could, with time and as required, make swords as well. But now we can no longer risk emergency **improvisation** of national defense; we have been compelled to create a permanent armaments industry of vast proportions. Added to this, three and a half million men and women are directly engaged in the defense establishment. We annually spend on military security more than the **net income** of all United States corporations.

armaments – military arms and equipment

plowshare – lower blade of an early plow. "Beat your swords into plowshares" is a Biblical plea for peace

improvise – create with whatever is available; perform without preparation

This **conjunction** of an immense military establishment and a large arms industry is new in the American experience. The total influence -- economic, political, even spiritual -- is felt in every city, every State house, every office of the Federal government.

net income – profit after expenses

conjunction – combination, happening together

We recognize the **imperative** need for this development. Yet we must not fail to comprehend its grave implications. Our toil, resources and livelihood are all involved; so is the very structure of our society.

imperative – crucial, of vital importance

In the councils of government, we must guard against the **acquisition** of unwarranted influence, whether sought or unsought, by the military industrial complex. The potential for the disastrous rise of misplaced power exists and will persist.

We must never let the weight of this combination endanger our liberties or democratic processes. We should take nothing for granted. Only an alert and knowledgeable citizenry can compel the proper meshing of the huge industrial and military machinery of defense with our peaceful methods and goals, so that security and liberty may prosper together.

Akin to, and largely responsible for the sweeping changes in our industrial-military **posture**, has been the technological revolution during recent decades.

In this revolution, research has become central; it also becomes more formalized, complex, and costly. A steadily increasing share is conducted for, by, or at the direction of, the Federal government.

Today, the solitary inventor, tinkering in his shop, has been overshadowed by task forces of scientists in laboratories and testing fields. In the same fashion, the free university, historically the **fountainhead** of free ideas and scientific discovery, has experienced a revolution in the conduct of research. Partly because of the huge costs involved, a government contract becomes virtually a substitute for intellectual curiosity. For every old blackboard there are now hundreds of new electronic computers.

The prospect of domination of the nation's scholars by Federal employment, project allocations, and the power of money is ever present and is **gravely** to be regarded. Yet, in holding scientific research and discovery in respect, as we should, we must also be alert to the equal and opposite danger that public policy could itself become the captive of a scientific technological elite.

It is the task of statesmanship to mold, to balance, and to integrate these and other forces, new and old, within the

acquisition– the act of getting or receiving of something

posture – capability in personnel and materiel that affect the capacity to fight a war

fountainhead– original or chief source

gravely – seriously or severely

principles of our democratic system -- ever aiming toward the supreme goals of our free society.

... **Disarmament**, with mutual honor and confidence, is a continuing imperative. Together we must learn how to compose differences, not with arms, but with intellect and decent purpose. Because this need is so sharp and apparent I confess that I lay down my official responsibilities in this field with a definite sense of disappointment. As one who has witnessed the horror and the lingering sadness of war -- as one who knows that another war could utterly destroy this civilization which has been so slowly and painfully built over thousands of years -- I wish I could say tonight that a lasting peace is in sight.

disarmament – reduction or withdrawal of military forces and weapons

Happily, I can say that war has been avoided. Steady progress toward our ultimate goal has been made. But, so much remains to be done. As a private citizen, I shall never cease to do what little I can to help the world advance along that road.

So -- in this my last good night to you as your President -- I thank you for the many opportunities you have given me for public service in war and peace...

Eisenhower's Farewell Address

1. Eisenhower claims that blackboards have been replaced by:
   A. think tanks
   B. computers
   C. task forces of scientists

2. Eisenhower says a safeguard of peace is a strong:
   A. military establishment
   B. American economy
   C. armaments industry

3. Eisenhower is most concerned here with:
   A. enemy threats
   B. the cost of war
   C. military and industrial influence

4. Eisenhower warns of a threat to:
   A. university budgets
   B. independent research
   C. presidential power

5. Eisenhower sees international differences as best dealt with by:
   A. disarmament
   B. peace treaties
   C. intellect

6. The word "*imperative*" as used in the passage (¶ 4) most nearly means:
   A. commanding
   B. essential
   C. unstoppable

7. The U.S. is said to spend more on military security than:
   A. any nation in the world
   B. the profits of all U.S. corporations
   C. all the wealth housed in Ft. Knox

8. Technological research is said to be mostly carried out by the:
   A. U.S. military
   B. U.S. corporations
   C. U.S. government

9. Reflecting on his own horrific wartime experience, Eisenhower believes:
   A. a lasting peace may be at hand
   B. civilization could be threatened
   C. progress has been made in avoiding war

10. Eisenhower says he is leaving office with a feeling of:
    A. hope
    B. disappointment
    C. pride

William Faulkner's Nobel Prize speech
At the Nobel Banquet at City Hall in Stockholm, December 10, 1950

Ladies and gentlemen,

I feel that this **award** was not made to me as a man, but to my work - a life's work in the agony and sweat of the human spirit, not for glory and least of all for profit, but to create out of the materials of the human spirit something which did not exist before. So this award is only mine in trust. It will not be difficult to find a dedication for the money part of it **commensurate** with the purpose and significance of its origin. But I would like to do the same with the **acclaim** too, by using this moment as a **pinnacle** from which I might be listened to by the young men and women already dedicated to the same anguish and **travail**, among whom is already that one who will someday stand here where I am standing.

Our tragedy today is a general and universal physical fear so long sustained by now that we can even bear it. There are no longer problems of the spirit. There is only the question: When will I be blown up? Because of this, the young man or woman writing today has forgotten the problems of the human heart in conflict with itself which alone can make good writing because only that is worth writing about, worth the agony and the sweat.

He must learn them again. He must teach himself that the basest of all things is to be afraid; and, teaching himself that, forget it forever, leaving no room in his workshop for anything but the old **verities** and truths of the heart, the old universal truths lacking which any story is **ephemeral** and doomed - love and honor and pity and pride and compassion and sacrifice. Until he does so, he labors under a curse. He writes not of love but of lust, of defeats in which nobody loses anything of value, of victories without hope and, worst of all, without pity or compassion. His griefs grieve on no universal bones, leaving no scars. He writes not of the heart but of the **glands**.

Until he relearns these things, he will write as though he stood among and watched the end of man. I decline to accept

William Faulkner
– Southern American writer, Pulitzer Prize winner, Nobelist

award – given in 1950 worth $2.96 million in today's dollars

commensurate – equal in measure or extent, corresponding in size

acclaim – enthusiastic approval, praise

pinnacle – highest point, peak

travail – anguish, suffering, labor with pain

verities – truths, realities, accordances with fact

ephemeral – lasting only a short time, fleeting, transitory, short-lived

glands – figurative: bodily reactions, such as sweat, tears, pains

the end of man. It is easy enough to say that man is immortal simply because he will endure: that when the last dingdong of doom has clanged and faded from the last worthless rock hanging tideless in the last red and dying evening, that even then there will still be one more sound: that of his puny inexhaustible voice, still talking.

I refuse to accept this. I believe that man will not merely endure: he will **prevail**. He is immortal, not because he alone among creatures has an inexhaustible voice, but because he has a soul, a spirit capable of compassion and sacrifice and endurance. The poet's, the writer's, duty is to write about these things. It is his privilege to help man endure by lifting his heart, by reminding him of the courage and honor and hope and pride and compassion and pity and sacrifice which have been the glory of his past. The poet's voice need not merely be the record of man, it can be one of the props, the pillars to help him endure and prevail.

prevail – triumph, win out, prove superior, succeed, exist widely

William Faulkner – Nobel Prize speech

1. Faulkner sees the award as recognition of his:
    A. literary mastery
    B. unique artistry
    C. life's contribution

2. The speech is being delivered in:
    A. Washington, D.C.
    B. Oslo, Norway
    C. Stockholm, Sweden

3. The author seeks to dedicate his award to encouraging:
    A. young writers
    B. human rights
    C. freedom of expression

4. Faulkner says the largest problem of current times is:
    A. existential fear
    B. spiritual weakness
    C. emotional complacency

5. For a literary work to last, it must deal with:
    A. problems of the common man
    B. enduring truths
    C. the record of human history

6. Faulkner's ultimate view of humanity is:
    A. optimistic
    B. skeptical
    C. fearful

7. Faulkner believes that writing that lasts is based on:
    A. gut instincts
    B. universal truths
    C. grief

8. The author believes that man is immortal so long as:
    A. he admits no defeat
    B. he endures through time
    C. his voice endures

9. Faulkner criticizes those authors who write from:
    A. desperation
    B. the heart
    C. the glands

10. The monetary value of Faulkner's Nobel Prize in today's currency is:
    A. $1 million
    B. $2 million
    C. $3 million

Faust
Johann Wolfgang von Goethe 1808

Johann Wolfgang von Goethe – [Guh-tuh] German writer, stateman, scientist [Text translation by Project Gutenberg]

In this opening monologue of a drama in rhymed verse, medieval scholar Faust reveals frustration with his academic life and hot desire to experience fully the wider and more mystical world – with the aid of the devil, Mephistopheles.

FAUST: Ah! Now I've done Philosophy,

I've finished Law and Medicine,

And sadly even Theology:

Taken fierce pains, from end to end.

Now here I am, a fool for sure!

No wiser than I was before:

Master, Doctor's what they call me,

And I've been ten years, already,

Crosswise, arcing, to and fro,

Leading my students by the nose,

And see that we can know - nothing!

It almost sets my heart burning.

I'm cleverer than all these teachers,

Doctors, Masters, scribes, preachers:

I'm not plagued by doubt or **scruple**,

Scared by neither Hell nor Devil –

Instead all Joy is snatched away,

What's worth knowing, I can't say,

Master – title of respect for a teacher, accomplished academician

scruple – mental reservation, reluctance on moral grounds

I can't say what I should teach

To make men better or convert each.

And then I've neither goods nor gold,

No worldly honour, or splendour hold:

Not even a dog would play this part!

So I've given myself to Magic art,

To see if, through Spirit powers and lips,

I might have all secrets at my fingertips.

And no longer, with **rancid** sweat, so,

Still have to speak what I cannot know:

That I may understand whatever

Binds the world's innermost core together,

See all its workings, and its seeds,

Deal no more in words' empty reeds.

rancid – having a rank smell; repugnant

Faust

1. What subject does Faust say he most regrets having studied?
    A. medicine
    B. philosophy
    C. religion

2. Faust has been teaching for:
    A. a decade
    B. half his life
    C. he can't recall

3. Faust is pained because he doesn't know:
    A. what's worth knowing
    B. what's left to study
    C. if life's worth living

4. Faust seems lately to have taken up:
    A. belief in an afterlife
    B. pagan ritualism
    C. black magic

5. Faust comes to the conclusion that he has become:
    A. boring
    B. too clever
    C. no wiser than before

6. The word *"scruple"* as used here most nearly means:
    A. hesitation
    B. experiment
    C. waste

7. Faust finally no longer wishes to be preoccupied with:
    A. lectures
    B. death
    C. words

8. Faust laments that he still speaks about:
    A. what he doesn't know
    B. Spirit powers
    C. secrets he can't reveal

9. Faust questions what he:
    A. should teach
    B. can look forward to
    C. believes in

10. Faust ranks himself lower than:
    A. the Devil
    B. a gambler
    C. a dog

Speech of His God and His Homeland
Geronimo (Goyathlay)   1906

The Apache Indians are divided into six subtribes. To one of these, the Be-don-ko-he, I belong. Our tribe inhabited that region of mountainous country which lies west from the east line of Arizona, and south from the head waters of the Gila River.

East of us lived the Chi-hen-ne (Ojo Caliente), (Hot Springs) Apaches. Our tribe never had any difficulty with them. Victoria, their chief, was always a friend to me. He always helped our tribe when we asked him for help. He lost his life in the defense of the rights of his people. He was a good man and a brave warrior. His son, Charlie, now lives here in this reservation with us. North of us lived the White Mountain Apaches. They were not always on the best of terms with our tribe, yet we seldom had any war with them. I knew their chief, Hash-ka-ai-la, personally, and I considered him a good warrior. Their **range** was next to that of the Navajo Indians, who were not of the same blood as the Apaches. We held councils with all Apache tribes, but never with the Navajo Indians. However, we traded with them and sometimes visited them. To the west of our country ranged the Chi-e-a-hen Apaches. They had two chiefs within my time, Co-si-to and Co-da-hoo-yah. They were friendly, but not **intimate** with our tribe.

South of us lived the Cho-kon-en (Chiricahua) Apaches, whose chief in the old days was <u>Cochise</u>, and later his son, Naiche. This tribe was always on the most friendly terms with us. We were often in camp and on the trail together. Naiche, who was my companion in arms, is now my companion in **bondage**. To the south and west of us lived the Ned-ni Apaches. Their chief was Whoa, called by the Mexicans Capitan Whoa. They were our firm friends. The land of this tribe lies partly in Old Mexico and partly in Arizona. Whoa and I often camped and fought side by side as brothers. My enemies were his enemies, my friends his friends. He is dead now, but his son Asa is interpreting this story for me. Still the four tribes (Bedonkohe, Chokonen, Chihenne, and Nedni), who were fast friends in the days of freedom, cling together

Geronimo – Apache chief whose wife, mother, and three children were murdered by Mexicans in 1858. He led his small band of raiders in revenge and resistance to tribal land encroachments by Mexico and Texas until, after a long pursuit, the warrior surrendered to Texan authorities as a war prisoner. Never allowed to return to his homeland, he died at Fort Sill, Oklahoma

range – area of roaming, scope of local geography

intimate – in a close or warm relationship

bondage – state of being a slave, captivity

as they decrease in number. Only the destruction of all our people would dissolve our bonds of friendship. We are vanishing from the earth, yet I cannot think we are useless or Usen would not have created us. He created all tribes of men and certainly had a **righteous** purpose in creating each. For each tribe of men Usen created, He also made a home. In the land created for any particular tribe, He placed whatever would be best for the welfare of that tribe.

righteous – in accord with divine or moral law

Usen created the Apaches. He also created their homes in the West. He gave to them such grain, fruits, and game as they needed to eat. To restore their health when disease attacked them, He made many different herbs to grow. He taught them where to find these herbs, and how to prepare them for medicine. He gave the Apaches a pleasant climate and all they needed for clothing and shelter was at hand. Thus it was in the beginning: the Apaches and their homes each created for the other by Usen himself. When they are taken from these homes they sicken and die. How long will it be until it is said, there are no Apaches?

We are now held on Comanche and Kiowa lands, which are not suited to our needs—these lands and this climate are suited to the Indians who originally inhabited this country, of course, but our people are decreasing in numbers here, and will continue to decrease unless they are allowed to return to their native land. Such a result is inevitable.

There is no climate or soil which, to my mind, is equal to that of Arizona. We could have plenty of good cultivating land, plenty of grass, plenty of timber and plenty of minerals in that land which the Almighty created for the Apaches. It is my land, my home, my fathers' land, to which I now ask to be allowed to return. I want to spend my last days there, and be buried among those mountains. If this could be I might die in peace, feeling that my people, placed in their native homes, would increase in numbers, rather than diminish as at present, and that our name would not become extinct.

I know that if my people were placed in that mountainous region lying around the headwaters of the Gila River they would live in peace and act according to the will of the

President. They would be prosperous and happy in tilling the soil and learning the civilization of the white men, whom they now respect. Could I but see this accomplished, I think I could forget all the wrongs that I have ever received, and die a contented and happy old man. But we can do nothing in this matter ourselves—we must wait until those in authority choose to act. If this cannot be done during my lifetime—if I must die in bondage—I hope that the remnant of the Apache tribe may, when I am gone, be granted the one privilege which they request—to return to Arizona.

— *Goyathlay (**Geronimo**) (1829-1909)*
Chiricahua Chief, Bedonkohe Band
Apache Nation

Geronimo – acquired that nickname during a battle with Mexican soldiers

Geronimo's Speech

1. Geronimo writes as a member of this tribal group:
    A. Chiricahua
    B. Comanche
    C. Navajo

2. At the time of this writing, Geronimo is:
    A. in a Florida prison
    B. on a home reservation
    C. on a foreign reservation

3. Geronimo's attitude toward the U.S. Government is:
    A. hostile
    B. grateful
    C. neither A nor B

4. "*Usen*" is what Germino's people call:
    A. their God
    B. the white man
    C. their native Arizona ground

5. Geronimo says his greatest wish now is:
    A. peace with the white man
    B. return to Arizona
    C. rejoining his warriors

6. The word "*bondage*" as used in the passage most nearly means:
    A. slavery
    B. brotherhood
    C. debt

7. Geronimo's speech is being communicated by this man as interpreter:
    A. Asa, son of Whoa
    B. Naiche, son of Cochise
    C. Charlie, son of Victoria

8. Geronimo says his people are threatened with extinction if:
    A. they are again hunted by the U.S. cavalry
    B. their reservation is closed
    C. they are barred from a return home

9. Geronimo says his people now regard the white man:
    A. with respect
    B. as fellowman
    C. with fear

10. Geronimo would be at peace if:
    A. the whites' admitted their wrongs
    B. his tribe returned to Arizona
    C. his burial was in Arizona

The Gift of the Magi
O. Henry, pen name of William Sydney Porter 1906

One dollar and eighty-seven cents. That was all. And sixty cents of it was in pennies. Pennies saved one and two at a time by bulldozing the grocer and the vegetable man and the butcher until one's cheeks burned with the silent **imputation** of **parsimony** that such close dealing implied. Three times Della counted it. One dollar and eighty-seven cents. And the next day would be Christmas.

There was clearly nothing to do but flop down on the shabby little couch and howl. So Della did it. Which **instigates** the moral reflection that life is made up of sobs, sniffles, and smiles, with sniffles predominating.

While the mistress of the home is gradually subsiding from the first stage to the second, take a look at the home. A furnished **flat** at $8 per week. It did not exactly beggar description, but it certainly had that word on the lookout for the **mendicancy** squad.

In the **vestibule** below was a letter-box into which no letter would go, and an electric button from which no mortal finger could coax a ring. Also **appertaining** thereunto was a card bearing the name "Mr. James Dillingham Young."

The "Dillingham" had been flung to the breeze during a former period of prosperity when its possessor was being paid $30 per week. Now, when the income was shrunk to $20, though, they were thinking seriously of contracting to a modest and unassuming D. But whenever Mr. James Dillingham Young came home and reached his flat above he was called "Jim" and greatly hugged by Mrs. James Dillingham Young, already introduced to you as Della. Which is all very good.

Della finished her cry and attended to her cheeks with the powder rag. She stood by the window and looked out dully at a gray cat walking a gray fence in a gray backyard. Tomorrow would be Christmas Day, and she had only $1.87 with which to buy Jim a present. She had been saving every

O. Henry – prodigious short story writer known for his wit

impute – attribute, insinuate, ascribe

parsimony – frugality, thrift, carefulness with money or resources

instigate – cause something to happen, initiate, begin

flat – an apartment on one floor of a building

mendicancy – poverty, pennilessness

vestibule – foyer, enclosed entryway

appertain – be a part or attribute of, belonging

penny she could for months, with this result. Twenty dollars a week doesn't go far. Expenses had been greater than she had calculated. They always are. Only $1.87 to buy a present for Jim. Her Jim. Many a happy hour she had spent planning for something nice for him. Something fine and rare and **sterling**--something just a little bit near to being worthy of the honor of being owned by Jim.

There was a **pier-glass** between the windows of the room. Perhaps you have seen a pier-glass in an $8 flat. A very thin and very agile person may, by observing his reflection in a rapid sequence of longitudinal strips, obtain a fairly accurate conception of his looks. Della, being slender, had mastered the art.

Suddenly she whirled from the window and stood before the glass. Her eyes were shining brilliantly, but her face had lost its color within twenty seconds. Rapidly she pulled down her hair and let it fall to its full length.

Now, there were two possessions of the James Dillingham Youngs in which they both took a mighty pride. One was Jim's gold watch that had been his father's and his grandfather's. The other was Della's hair. Had the **queen of Sheba** lived in the flat across the airshaft, Della would have let her hair hang out the window some day to dry just to **depreciate** Her Majesty's jewels and gifts. Had **King Solomon** been the janitor, with all his treasures piled up in the basement, Jim would have pulled out his watch every time he passed, just to see him pluck at his beard from envy.

So now Della's beautiful hair fell about her rippling and shining like a cascade of brown waters. It reached below her knee and made itself almost a garment for her. And then she did it up again nervously and quickly. Once she faltered for a minute and stood still while a tear or two splashed on the worn red carpet.

On went her old brown jacket; on went her old brown hat. With a whirl of skirts and with the brilliant sparkle still in her

sterling – conforming to the highest standard

pier-glass – tall mirror placed between windows

Sheba – wealthy Arabian queen who visited and exchanged gifts with Solomon

depreciate – diminish in value, belittle

King Solomon – Biblical ruler of Israel renowned for his wisdom and wealth

eyes, she fluttered out the door and down the stairs to the street.

Where she stopped the sign read: "**Mne. Sofronie**. Hair Goods of All Kinds." One flight up Della ran, and collected herself, panting. Madame, large, too white, chilly, hardly looked the "Sofronie."

"Will you buy my hair?" asked Della.

"I buy hair," said Madame. "Take yer hat off and let's have a sight at the looks of it."

Down rippled the brown cascade.

"Twenty dollars," said Madame, lifting the mass with a practised hand.

"Give it to me quick," said Della.

Oh, and the next two hours tripped by on rosy wings. Forget the hashed metaphor. She was **ransacking** the stores for Jim's present.

She found it at last. It surely had been made for Jim and no one else. There was no other like it in any of the stores, and she had turned all of them inside out. It was a platinum **fob** chain simple and **chaste** in design, properly proclaiming its value by substance alone and not by **meretricious** ornamentation--as all good things should do. It was even worthy of The Watch. As soon as she saw it she knew that it must be Jim's. It was like him. Quietness and value--the description applied to both. Twenty-one dollars they took from her for it, and times looked at it on the sly on account of the old leather strap that he used in place of a chain. When Della reached home her intoxication gave way a little to **prudence** and reason. She got out her curling irons and lighted the gas and went to work repairing the ravages made by generosity added to love. Which is always a tremendous task, dear friends--a mammoth task.

Mne. – properly should be **M<u>me</u>** as the abbreviation for the French title 'madame'

Sofronie – suggests that this woman is using a false name to make herself sound foreign, aristocratic, and exotic

ransacking – searching or examining thoroughly

fob – pocket watch chain

chaste – simple in design, unadorned

meretricious – cheap, trashy, tasteless

prudence – caution, good judgment

Within forty minutes her head was covered with tiny, close-lying curls that made her look wonderfully like a **truant** schoolboy. She looked at her reflection in the mirror long, carefully, and critically.

"If Jim doesn't kill me," she said to herself, "before he takes a second look at me, he'll say I look like a **Coney Island chorus girl**. But what could I do--oh! what could I do with a dollar and eighty-seven cents?"

At 7 o'clock the coffee was made and the frying-pan was on the back of the stove hot and ready to cook the chops.

Jim was never late. Della doubled the fob chain in her hand and sat on the corner of the table near the door that he always entered. Then she heard his step on the stair away down on the first flight, and she turned white for just a moment. She had a habit for saying little silent prayer about the simplest everyday things, and now she whispered: "Please God, make him think I am still pretty."

The door opened and Jim stepped in and closed it. He looked thin and very serious. Poor fellow, he was only twenty-two--and to be burdened with a family! He needed a new overcoat and he was without gloves.

Jim stopped inside the door, as immovable as a **setter** at the scent of **quail**. His eyes were fixed upon Della, and there was an expression in them that she could not read, and it terrified her. It was not anger, nor surprise, nor disapproval, nor horror, nor any of the sentiments that she had been prepared for. He simply stared at her fixedly with that peculiar expression on his face.

Della wriggled off the table and went for him.

"Jim, darling," she cried, "don't look at me that way. I had my hair cut off and sold because I couldn't have lived through Christmas without giving you a present. It'll grow out again--you won't mind, will you? I just had to do it. My hair grows awfully fast. Say `Merry Christmas!' Jim, and let's be happy.

truant – student skipping school

Coney Island – NY amusement park

chorus girl – singer or dancer of the chorus in a musical show

setter – a hunting dog breed

quail – game bird like a partridge

You don't know what a nice-- what a beautiful, nice gift I've got for you."

"You've cut off your hair?" asked Jim, laboriously, as if he had not arrived at that patent fact yet even after the hardest mental labor.

"Cut it off and sold it," said Della. "Don't you like me just as well, anyhow? I'm me without my hair, ain't I?"

Jim looked about the room curiously.

"You say your hair is gone?" he said, with an air almost of idiocy.

"You needn't look for it," said Della. "It's sold, I tell you--sold and gone, too. It's Christmas Eve, boy. Be good to me, for it went for you. Maybe the hairs of my head were numbered," she went on with sudden serious sweetness, "but nobody could ever count my love for you. Shall I put the chops on, Jim?"

Out of his trance Jim seemed quickly to wake. He enfolded his Della. For ten seconds let us regard with **discreet** scrutiny some **inconsequential** object in the other direction. Eight dollars a week or a million a year--what is the difference? A mathematician or a **wit** would give you the wrong answer. The magi brought valuable gifts, but that was not among them. This dark assertion will be illuminated later on.

"Don't make any mistake, Dell," he said, "about me. I don't think there's anything in the way of a haircut or a shave or a shampoo that could make me like my girl any less. But if you'll unwrap that package you may see why you had me going a while at first."

White fingers and nimble tore at the string and paper. And then an ecstatic scream of joy; and then, alas! a quick feminine change to hysterical tears and wails, necessitating the immediate employment of all the comforting powers of the lord of the flat.

discreet – modest, prudent

inconsequential – not important or significant

wit – a person with a talent for using words and ideas in a quick and inventive way

For there lay The Combs--the set of combs, side and back, that Della had worshipped long in a Broadway window. Beautiful combs, pure tortoise shell, with jewelled rims--just the shade to wear in the beautiful vanished hair. They were expensive combs, she knew, and her heart had simply craved and yearned over them without the least hope of possession. And now, they were hers, but the **tresses** that should have adorned the coveted adornments were gone.

tresses – long unbound hair of a woman

But she hugged them to her bosom, and at length she was able to look up with dim eyes and a smile and say: "My hair grows so fast, Jim!"

And then Della leaped up like a little **singed** cat and cried, "Oh, oh!"

singed [sinjd] – lightly or superficially burned

Jim had not yet seen his beautiful present. She held it out to him eagerly upon her open palm. The dull precious metal seemed to flash with a reflection of her bright and ardent spirit.

"Isn't it a dandy, Jim? I hunted all over town to find it. You'll have to look at the time a hundred times a day now. Give me your watch. I want to see how it looks on it."

Instead of obeying, Jim tumbled down on the couch and put his hands under the back of his head and smiled.

"Dell," said he, "let's put our Christmas presents away and keep 'em a while. They're too nice to use just at present. I sold the watch to get the money to buy your combs. And now suppose you put the chops on."

The magi, as you know, were wise men--wonderfully wise men--who brought gifts to the Babe in the **manger**. They invented the art of giving Christmas presents. Being wise, their gifts were no doubt wise ones, possibly bearing the privilege of exchange in case of duplication. And here I have lamely related to you the uneventful **chronicle** of two foolish children in a flat who most unwisely sacrificed for each other the greatest treasures of their house. But in a last word to the

manger – trough or open box from which horses or cattle are fed

chronicle – factual, detail record of important or historical events

82

wise of these days let it be said that of all who give gifts these two were the wisest. O all who give and receive gifts, such as they are wisest. Everywhere they are wisest. They are the magi.

The Gift of the Magi

1. The story takes place:
    A. on Christmas Eve
    B. on Christmas Day
    C. two days before Christmas

2. Della is most worried about:
    A. a present for Jim
    B. loss of her hair
    C. their constant lack of money

3. It can be inferred that Madame Sofronie is a:
    A. hair stylist
    B. wig seller
    C. French native

4. Della goes home with this much money:
    A. $8.17
    B. $1.87
    C. $.87

5. The magi are referred to in association with their:
    A. wisdom
    B. travel
    C. gift giving

6. The word "*chaste*" as used in the passage most nearly means:
    A. virginal
    B. fleeting
    C. unadorned

7. Della's reaction to the Combs is compared to that of:
    A. a scorched cat
    B. the queen of Sheba
    C. a Coney Island chorus girl

8. "The greatest treasures of their house" (last ¶) are:
    A. their mutual affections
    B. what they sold
    C. their promise of a family

9. After their presents are opened, Jim suggests that they be:
    A. put away
    B. exchanged
    C. left under the tree

10. Della and Jim are as a pair compared to:
    A. foolish children
    B. the magi
    C. both A&B

Gladiators
Seneca 50 AD

The Roman philosopher Seneca, in a letter to a friend, describes what he saw in the arena during the reign of **Emperor Caligula**:

"There is nothing so ruinous to good character as to **idle away** one's time at some **spectacle**. Vices have a way of creeping in because of the feeling of pleasure that it brings. Why do you think that I say that I personally return from shows greedier, more ambitious and more given to luxury, and I might add, with thoughts of greater cruelty and less humanity, simply because I have been among humans?

The other day, I **chanced** to drop in at the midday games, expecting sport and **wit** and some relaxation to rest men's eyes from the sight of human blood. Just the opposite was the case. Any fighting before that was as nothing; all trifles were now put aside - it was plain butchery.

The men had nothing with which to protect themselves, for their whole bodies were open to the thrust, and every thrust told. The common people prefer this to matches on **level** terms or request performances. Of course they do. The blade is not **parried** by helmet or shield, and what use is skill or defense? All these merely postpone death.

In the morning men are thrown to bears or lions, at midday to those who were previously watching them. The crowd cries for the killers to be paired with those who will kill them, and reserves the victor for yet another death. This is the only release the gladiators have. The whole business needs fire and steel to urge men on to fight. There was no escape for them. The slayer was kept fighting until he could be slain.

'Kill him! Flog him! Burn him alive!' (the spectators roared) 'Why is he such a coward? Why won't he rush on the **steel**? Why does he fall so **meekly**? Why won't he die willingly? "

Unhappy as I am, how have I deserved that I must look on such a scene as this? Do not, my Lucilius, attend the games, I

Seneca – Roman Stoic philosopher, statesman, and dramatist

Caligula – reputedly cruel, sadistic, and perverse; first emperor to be assassinated 41 AD

idle away – waste, fritter, pass time

spectacle – dramatic public display or show

chanced – happened

wit – fun, pleasantry, play

level – fair, equal

parried – deflected, turned aside, evaded

steel – sharp weapon like a sword or spear

meekly – submissively, timidly

pray you. Either you will be corrupted by the multitude, or, if you show disgust, be hated by them. So stay away."

Gladiators

1. Seneca is reported in this passage to have been a:
   A. Senator
   B. philosopher
   C. commander

2. Seneca says that what makes him less human is:
   A. watching bloodshed
   B. wealth
   C. being among others

3. Seneca attends the arena in order to see:
   A. sports
   B. animal fighting
   C. blood being spilled

4. In the gladiatorial contests, Seneca says that the combatant adversaries often involve:
   A. unfair advantages
   B. unpredictability
   C. equally chosen competitors

5. The contests are taking place during the reign of:
   A. Augustus
   B. Nero
   C. Caligula

6. The common people are said to prefer gladiatorial contests in which combatants are:
   A. equal
   B. criminals
   C. unprotected

7. Seneca writes that an audience member's pleasure at the games derives from:
   A. vices
   B. blood lust
   C. spectacle

8. This letter is addressed to:
   A. the Senate
   B. Seneca's friend
   C. Seneca's son

9. Seneca warns that if Lucilius attends the games and shows disgust, he will:
   A. gradually be won over
   B. be corrupted
   C. be hated

10. Seneca's actual reaction to the games seems to be:
    A. fascination
    B. revulsion
    C. anger

John Brown's Final Words November 2, 1859

On October 16, 1859, **abolitionist** John Brown, his sons, and more than a dozen others seized the armory at Harper's Ferry, (West) Virginia, ostensibly to initiate and arm a slave uprising. Captured by troops commanded by Robert E. Lee, Brown was tried, found guilty of treason, and sentenced to hang. A month before his execution, Brown addressed the courtroom in Charleston, West Virginia, defending his actions.

abolitionist – person advocating doing away with or termination of slavery

I have, may it please the Court, a few words to say:

In the first place, I deny everything but what I have all along admitted, the **design** on my part to free the slaves. I intended certainly to have made a **clean** thing of that matter, as I did last winter, when I went into Missouri and there took slaves without the snapping of a gun on either side, moved them through the country, and finally left them in Canada. I designed to have done the same thing again, on a larger scale. That was all I intended. I never did intend murder, or treason, or the destruction of property, or to excite or incite slaves to rebellion, or to make **insurrection**.

design – intention, plan

clean – non-violent

I have another objection; and that is, it is unjust that I should suffer such a penalty. Had I interfered in the manner which I admit, and which I admit has been fairly proved (for I admire the truthfulness and **candor** of the greater portion of the witnesses who have testified in this case), had I so interfered in behalf of the rich, the powerful, the intelligent, the so-called great, or in behalf of any of their friends, either father, mother, brother, sister, wife, or children, or any of that class, and suffered and sacrificed what I have in this **interference**, it would have been all right; and every man in this court would have deemed it an act worthy of reward rather than punishment.

insurrection – revolt against civil authority, uprising, rebellion

candor – frankness, fairness, impartiality

interference – episode, disruption

This court acknowledges, as I **suppose**, the validity of the law of God. I see a book kissed here which I suppose to be the Bible, or at least the New Testament. That teaches me that all things whatsoever I would that men should do to me, I should do even so to them. It teaches me, further, to "remember them that are in bonds, as bound with them." I endeavored to act up to that instruction. I say, I am yet too young to understand

suppose – presume

that God is any respecter of persons. I believe that to have interfered as I have done as I have always freely admitted I have done in behalf of His despised poor, was not wrong, but right. Now, if it is deemed necessary that I should forfeit my life for the furtherance of the ends of justice, and mingle my blood further with the blood of my children and with the blood of millions in this slave country whose rights are disregarded by wicked, cruel, and unjust enactments, I submit; so let it be done!

Let me say one word further.

I feel entirely satisfied with the treatment I have received on my trial. Considering all the circumstances. it has been more generous than I expected. But I feel no consciousness of guilt. I have stated from the first what was my intention and what was not. I never had any design against the life of any person, nor any disposition to commit treason, or excite slaves to rebel, or make any general insurrection. I never encouraged any man to do so, but always discouraged any idea of that kind.

Let me say, also, a word in regard to the statements made by some of those connected with me. I hear it has been stated by some of them that I have induced them to join me. But the contrary is true.

I do not say this to injure them, but as regretting their weakness. There is not one of them but joined me of his own accord, and the greater part of them at their own expense. A number of them I never saw, and never had a word of conversation with, till the day they came to me; and that was for the purpose I have stated.

Now I have done.

Brown's last words, written on a note handed to a guard just before his hanging:

"I, John Brown, am now quite certain that the crimes of this guilty land can never be purged away but with blood."

John Brown's Final Words

1. Brown admits to earlier success in smuggling slaves to Canada from:
   A. Kansas
   B. Missouri
   C. Nebraska

2. Brown supports the federal accusations that his intent at Harper's Ferry was to:
   A. liberate slaves
   B. incite rebellion
   C. commit treason

3. The testimony of trial witnesses is viewed as fundamentally:
   A. trustworthy
   B. in the interest of the socially powerful
   C. prejudiced

4. Brown defends his actions by an appeal to:
   A. specific reading of the law
   B. the Bible
   C. righteousness

5. Brown expresses doubt about certain witnesses because they:
   A. acted in self-interest
   B. claimed Brown pressured them
   C. were unknown to him

6. The word *"insurrection"* in context (¶ 1) most nearly means:
   A. objection
   B. initiation
   C. uprising

7. Brown states that his aim in taking slaves in Missouri was to:
   A. incite their general revolt
   B. free them
   C. relocate them to Canada

8. Brown maintains that had he acted on behalf of the upper class rich and powerful, his act would be deemed:
   A. commendable
   B. despicable
   C. worthy of punishment

9. In defense of his actions, Brown cites the:
   A. Declaration of Independence
   B. Golden Rule
   C. Magna Carta

10. Brown says he is willing to forfeit his life for:
   A. justice
   B. abolition
   C. enlisting others in his cause

The Lady, or the Tiger?
Frank Stockton 1882

In the very olden time there lived a semi-barbaric king, whose ideas, though somewhat polished and sharpened by the progressiveness of distant Latin neighbors, were still large, **florid**, and **untrammeled**, as became the half of him which was barbaric. He was a man of **exuberant fancy**, and, **withal**, of an authority so irresistible that, at his will, he turned his varied fancies into facts. He was greatly given to **self-communing**, and, when he and himself agreed upon anything, the thing was done. When every member of his domestic and political systems moved smoothly in its appointed course, his nature was bland and **genial**; but, whenever there was a little hitch, and some of his orbs got out of their orbits, he was blander and more genial still, for nothing pleased him so much as to make the crooked straight and crush down uneven places.

Among the borrowed notions by which his barbarism had become **semified** was that of the public arena, in which, by exhibitions of manly and beastly valor, the minds of his subjects were refined and cultured.

But even here the **exuberant** and barbaric fancy asserted itself. The arena of the king was built, not to give the people an opportunity of hearing the **rhapsodies** of dying gladiators, nor to enable them to view the inevitable conclusion of a conflict between religious opinions and hungry jaws, but for purposes far better adapted to widen and develop the mental energies of the people. This vast amphitheater, with its encircling galleries, its mysterious vaults, and its unseen passages, was an agent of **poetic justice**, in which crime was punished, or virtue rewarded, by the decrees of an impartial and incorruptible chance.

When a subject was accused of a crime of sufficient importance to interest the king, public notice was given that on an appointed day the fate of the accused person would be decided in the king's arena, a structure which well deserved its name, for, although its form and plan were borrowed from afar, its purpose **emanated** solely from the brain of this man,

Frank Stockton – American writer and humorist, known for children's fairy tales

florid – intricate, ornate

untrammeled – unhindered

exuberant – gleeful

fancy – imagination

withal – besides

self-communing – day-dreaming

genial – pleasant

semified – reduced

exuberant – uninhibited, enthusiastic

rhapsodies – enthusiastic expressions of feeling

poetic justice – just desserts, fitting retribution

emanate – emerge, originate, derive

91

who, every **barleycorn** a king, knew no tradition to which he owed more allegiance than pleased his fancy, and who **ingrafted** on every adopted form of human thought and action the rich growth of his barbaric idealism.

When all the people had assembled in the galleries, and the king, surrounded by his court, sat high up on his throne of royal state on one side of the arena, he gave a signal, a door beneath him opened, and the accused subject stepped out into the amphitheater. Directly opposite him, on the other side of the enclosed space, were two doors, exactly alike and side by side. It was the duty and the privilege of the person on trial to walk directly to these doors and open one of them. He could open either door he pleased; he was subject to no guidance or influence but that of the aforementioned impartial and incorruptible chance. If he opened the one, there came out of it a hungry tiger, the fiercest and most cruel that could be procured, which immediately sprang upon him and tore him to pieces as a punishment for his guilt. The moment that the case of the criminal was thus decided, **doleful** iron bells were clanged, great wails went up from the hired mourners posted on the outer rim of the arena, and the vast audience, with bowed heads and downcast hearts, wended slowly their homeward way, mourning greatly that one so young and fair, or so old and respected, should have merited so dire a fate.

But, if the accused person opened the other door, there came forth from it a lady, the most suitable to his years and station that his majesty could select among his fair subjects, and to this lady he was immediately married, as a reward of his innocence. It mattered not that he might already possess a wife and family, or that his affections might be engaged upon an object of his own selection; the king allowed no such subordinate arrangements to interfere with his great scheme of **retribution** and reward. The exercises, as in the other instance, took place immediately, and in the arena. Another door opened beneath the king, and a priest, followed by a band of **choristers**, and dancing maidens blowing joyous airs on golden horns and treading an **epithalamic** measure, advanced to where the pair stood, side by side, and the wedding was promptly and cheerily solemnized. Then the gay

barleycorn – an old unit of length equal to a third of an inch

ingrafted – incorporated, grafted onto another plant

doleful – very sad, full of grief

retribution – recompense, punishment given in repayment

chorister – singer in a choir

epithalamic – like a marriage song

brass bells rang forth their merry peals, the people shouted glad hurrahs, and the innocent man, preceded by children strewing flowers on his path, led his bride to his home.

This was the king's semi-barbaric method of administering justice. Its perfect fairness is obvious. The criminal could not know out of which door would come the lady; he opened either he pleased, without having the slightest idea whether, in the next instant, he was to be devoured or married. On some occasions the tiger came out of one door, and on some out of the other. The decisions of this **tribunal** were not only fair, they were positively determinate: the accused person was instantly punished if he found himself guilty, and, if innocent, he was rewarded on the spot, whether he liked it or not. There was no escape from the judgments of the king's arena.

tribunal – court of justice

The institution was a very popular one. When the people gathered together on one of the great trial days, they never knew whether they were to witness a bloody slaughter or a **hilarious** wedding. This element of uncertainty lent an interest to the occasion which it could not otherwise have attained. Thus, the masses were entertained and pleased, and the thinking part of the community could bring no charge of unfairness against this plan, for did not the accused person have the whole matter in his own hands?

hilarious – causing great merriment

This semi-barbaric king had a daughter as blooming as his most florid fancies, and with a soul as **fervent** and **imperious** as his own. As is usual in such cases, she was the apple of his eye, and was loved by him above all humanity. Among his courtiers was a young man of that fineness of blood and lowness of station common to the conventional heroes of romance who love royal maidens. This royal maiden was well satisfied with her lover, for he was handsome and brave to a degree unsurpassed in all this kingdom, and she loved him with an **ardor** that had enough of barbarism in it to make it exceedingly warm and strong. This love affair moved on happily for many months, until one day the king happened to discover its existence. He did not hesitate nor waver in regard to his duty in the premises. The youth was immediately cast into prison, and a day was appointed for his trial in the king's arena. This, of course, was an especially important occasion,

fervent – passionate, intense, enthusiastic

imperious – dictatorial, overbearing

ardor – great warmth of feeling, fervor

and his majesty, as well as all the people, was greatly interested in the workings and development of this trial. Never before had such a case occurred; never before had a subject dared to love the daughter of the king. In after years such things became commonplace enough, but then they were in no slight degree **novel** and startling.

novel – new and different, unusual

The tiger-cages of the kingdom were searched for the most savage and relentless beasts, from which the fiercest monster might be selected for the arena; and the ranks of maiden youth and beauty throughout the land were carefully surveyed by competent judges in order that the young man might have a fitting bride in case fate did not determine for him a different destiny. Of course, everybody knew that the deed with which the accused was charged had been done. He had loved the princess, and neither he, she, nor anyone else, thought of denying the fact; but the king would not think of allowing any fact of this kind to interfere with the workings of the tribunal, in which he took such great delight and satisfaction. No matter how the affair turned out, the youth would be disposed of, and the king would take an **aesthetic** pleasure in watching the course of events, which would determine whether or not the young man had done wrong in allowing himself to love the princess.

aesthetic – sense of the beautiful, pleasure in appearance

The appointed day arrived. From far and near the people gathered, and thronged the great galleries of the arena, and crowds, unable to gain admittance, massed themselves against its outside walls. The king and his court were in their places, opposite the twin doors, those fateful **portals**, so terrible in their similarity.

portal – door, entrance

All was ready. The signal was given. A door beneath the royal party opened, and the lover of the princess walked into the arena. Tall, beautiful, fair, his appearance was greeted with a low hum of admiration and anxiety. Half the audience had not known so grand a youth had lived among them. No wonder the princess loved him! What a terrible thing for him to be there!

As the youth advanced into the arena he turned, as the custom was, to bow to the king, but he did not think at all of that royal personage. His eyes were fixed upon the princess, who sat to the right of her father. Had it not been for the **moiety** of barbarism in her nature it is probable that lady would not have been there, but her intense and fervid soul would not allow her to be absent on an occasion in which she was so terribly interested. From the moment that the decree had gone forth that her lover should decide his fate in the king's arena, she had thought of nothing, night or day, but this great event and the various subjects connected with it. Possessed of more power, influence, and force of character than any one who had ever before been interested in such a case, she had done what no other person had done - she had possessed herself of the secret of the doors. She knew in which of the two rooms, that lay behind those doors, stood the cage of the tiger, with its open front, and in which waited the lady. Through these thick doors, heavily curtained with skins on the inside, it was impossible that any noise or suggestion should come from within to the person who should approach to raise the latch of one of them. But gold, and the power of a woman's will, had brought the secret to the princess.

And not only did she know in which room stood the lady ready to emerge, all blushing and radiant, should her door be opened, but she knew who the lady was. It was one of the fairest and loveliest of the **damsels** of the court who had been selected as the reward of the accused youth, should he be proved innocent of the crime of **aspiring** to one so far above him; and the princess hated her. Often had she seen, or imagined that she had seen, this fair creature throwing glances of admiration upon the person of her lover, and sometimes she thought these glances were perceived, and even returned. Now and then she had seen them talking together; it was but for a moment or two, but much can be said in a brief space; it may have been on most unimportant topics, but how could she know that? The girl was lovely, but she had dared to raise her eyes to the loved one of the princess; and, with all the intensity of the savage blood transmitted to her through long lines of wholly barbaric ancestors, she hated the woman who blushed and trembled behind that silent door.

moiety – portion, share

damsel – young unmarried noblewoman

aspiring – strongly desiring, striving after

95

When her lover turned and looked at her, and his eye met hers as she sat there, paler and whiter than anyone in the vast ocean of anxious faces about her, he saw, by that power of quick perception which is given to those whose souls are one, that she knew behind which door crouched the tiger, and behind which stood the lady. He had expected her to know it. He understood her nature, and his soul was assured that she would never rest until she had made plain to herself this thing, hidden to all other lookers-on, even to the king. The only hope for the youth in which there was any element of certainty was based upon the success of the princess in discovering this mystery; and the moment he looked upon her, he saw she had succeeded, as in his soul he knew she would succeed.

Then it was that his quick and anxious glance asked the question: "Which?" It was as plain to her as if he shouted it from where he stood. There was not an instant to be lost. The question was asked in a flash; it must be answered in another.

Her right arm lay on the cushioned **parapet** before her. She raised her hand, and made a slight, quick movement toward the right. No one but her lover saw her. Every eye but his was fixed on the man in the arena.

parapet – rampart, protective wall

He turned, and with a firm and rapid step he walked across the empty space. Every heart stopped beating, every breath was held, every eye was fixed immovably upon that man. Without the slightest hesitation, he went to the door on the right, and opened it.

Now, the point of the story is this: Did the tiger come out of that door, or did the lady?

The more we reflect upon this question, the harder it is to answer. It involves a study of the human heart which leads us through devious mazes of passion, out of which it is difficult to find our way. Think of it, fair reader, not as if the decision of the question depended upon yourself, but upon that hot-blooded, semi-barbaric princess, her soul at a white heat beneath the combined fires of despair and jealousy. She had lost him, but who should have him?

How often, in her waking hours and in her dreams, had she started in wild horror, and covered her face with her hands as she thought of her lover opening the door on the other side of which waited the cruel fangs of the tiger!

But how much oftener had she seen him at the other door! How in her grievous **reveries** had she gnashed her teeth, and torn her hair, when she saw his start of **rapturous** delight as he opened the door of the lady! How her soul had burned in agony when she had seen him rush to meet that woman, with her flushing cheek and sparkling eye of triumph; when she had seen him lead her forth, his whole frame kindled with the joy of recovered life; when she had heard the glad shouts from the multitude, and the wild ringing of the happy bells; when she had seen the priest, with his joyous followers, advance to the couple, and make them man and wife before her very eyes; and when she had seen them walk away together upon their path of flowers, followed by the tremendous shouts of the hilarious multitude, in which her one despairing shriek was lost and drowned!

reveries – daydreams

rapturous – expressing great pleasure

Would it not be better for him to die at once, and go to wait for her in the blessed regions of semi-barbaric futurity?

And yet, that awful tiger, those shrieks, that blood!

Her decision had been indicated in an instant, but it had been made after days and nights of anguished **deliberation**. She had known she would be asked, she had decided what she would answer, and, without the slightest hesitation, she had moved her hand to the right.

deliberation – careful consideration before a decision

The question of her decision is one not to be lightly considered, and it is not for me to presume to set myself up as the one person able to answer it. And so I leave it with all of you: Which came out of the opened door – the lady, or the tiger?

The Lady, or the Tiger?

1. At the end of this story, this appears from behind the door of the king's amphitheater:
    A. a lady
    B. a tiger
    C. either A or B

2. The man challenged in the arena is a young:
    A. prince
    B. gladiator
    C. criminal

3. The king is described as:
    A. arrogant
    B. excitable
    C. a daydreamer

4. The main stated purpose of the amphitheater is as a place to:
    A. administer justice
    B. showcase blood sports
    C. assemble the citizenry

5. Behind one door is a woman whom the chooser:
    A. can set free
    B. must immediately marry
    C. wins as a slave

6. The king's daughter has learned the identity of the lady behind one of the doors. The princess subsequently feels:
    A. hatred
    B. relief
    C. amusement

7. The young man's selection of doors is based on:
    A. a signal from the princess
    B. his advance knowledge through bribery
    C. random chance

8. The word "*novel*" (p.94) as used in the passage most nearly means:
    A. non-fiction
    B. atypical
    C. imaginary

9. The genre of this story is best described as:
    A. a fairy tale
    B. a fable
    C. heroic

10. The king compels the prisoner to the choice ordeal because the prisoner is:
    A. a common criminal
    B. his daughter's lover
    C. a threat

Letter from Hernan Cortes 1519

The conquistador Hernan Cortes describes the reaction of King Moctezuma to the Spaniard's entry into the **Aztec** capital.

Close to the city there is a wooden bridge ten paces wide across a breach in the **causeway** to allow the water to flow, as it rises and falls. After we had crossed this bridge, Moctezuma came to greet us and with him some two hundred lords, all barefoot and dressed in a different costume, but also very rich in their way and more so than the others. They came in two columns, pressed very close to the walls of the street, which is very wide and beautiful and so straight that you can see from one end to the other. It is two-thirds of a **league** long and has on both sides very good and big houses, both dwellings and temples.

Moctezuma came down the middle of this street with two chiefs, one on his right hand and the other on his left. When we met I dismounted and stepped forward to embrace him, but the two lords who were with him stopped me with their hands so that I should not touch him; and they likewise all performed the ceremony of kissing the earth. When at last I came to speak to Moctezuma himself I took off a necklace of pearls and cut glass that I was wearing and placed it round his neck; after we had walked a little way up the street a servant of his came with two necklaces, wrapped in a cloth, made from red snails' shells, which they hold in great **esteem**; and from each necklace hung eight shrimps of refined gold almost a span in length. And after he had given me these things he sat on another throne which they placed there next to the one on which I was sitting, and addressed me in the following way:

"For a long time we have known from the writings of our ancestors that neither I [Moctezuma], nor any of those who dwell in this land, are natives of it, but foreigners who came from very distant parts; and likewise we know that a chieftain, of whom they were all **vassals**, brought our people to this region. And he returned to his native land and after many years came again, by which time all those who had remained were married to native women and had

Hernan Cortes – 16th century Spanish conqueror/destroyer of the Aztec civilization

Aztec – 15th-16th century civilization of northern Mexico

causeway – a raised way across wet ground or water

league – unit of distance of about 3 miles

esteem – respect, admiration

vassals – those in a subservient or subordinate position a subject

99

built villages and raised children. And when he wished to lead them away again they would not go nor even admit him as their chief, and so he departed. And we have always held that those who descended from him would come and conquer this land and take us as their vassals. So because of the place from which you claim to come, namely, from where the sun rises, and the things you tell us of the great lord or king who sent you here, we believe and are certain that he is our natural lord, especially as you say that he has known of us for some time. So be assured that we shall obey you and hold you as our lord in place of that great **sovereign** of whom you speak; and in this there shall be no offense or betrayal whatsoever. I know full well of all that has happened to you from **Puntunchan** to here, and I also know how those of **Cempoal** and **Tascalteca** have told you much evil of me; believe only what you see with your eyes, for those are my enemies, and some were my vassals, and have rebelled against me at your coming and said those things to gain favor with you. I also know that they have told you the walls of my houses are, made of gold, and that the floor mats in my rooms and other things in my household are likewise of gold, and that I was, and claimed to be, a god; and many other things besides. The houses as you see are of stone and lime and clay."

sovereign – supreme ruler, monarch

Puntunchan, Cempoal, Tascalteca – Aztec cities

Then he raised his clothes and showed me his body, saying, as he grasped his arms and trunk with his hands, "See that I am of flesh and blood like you and all other men, and I am mortal and substantial. See how they have lied to you? It is true that I have some pieces of gold left to me by my ancestors; anything I might have shall be given to you whenever you ask. Now I shall go to other houses where I live, but here you shall be provided with all that you and your people require, and you shall receive no hurt, for you are in your own land and your own house."

Letter from Hernan Cortes

1. Cortes' attitude toward King Moctezuma reflects the Spanish Conquistador's:
    A. respect
    B. greed
    C. hostility

2. The people Cortes is writing about here are:
    A. Mayan
    B. Incan
    C. Aztec

3. Moctezuma reacts to Cortes with:
    A. suspicion
    B. generosity
    C. worship

4. The encounter takes place in current day:
    A. Peru
    B. Mexico
    C. Guatemala

5. Those accompanying Moctezuma all show their respect by:
    A. bowing their heads
    B. kissing the ground
    C. chanting his name

6. The two men exchange gifts of:
    A. gold
    B. clothing
    C. necklaces

7. The word "*vassal*" as used in the passage most nearly refers to a:
    A. king
    B. captive
    C. subordinate

8. Cortes notes that a type of this item seems highly prized by his hosts:
    A. turquoise
    B. snail shells
    C. pearls

9. Cortes listens to Moctezuma's narrative while the Spaniard is seated on:
    A. his horse
    B. a throne
    C. a terrace

10. Moctezuma insists that:
    A. the walls of his house are made of gold
    B. he is a god
    C. his people will treat Cortes as their lord

Liberty or Death

Patrick Henry – a speech delivered before the Virginia Convention of Delegates at St. John's Church, Richmond, Virginia, March 23, 1775

Patrick Henry – American attorney, politician, and orator who advocated Virginia independence in 1770s

Mr. President:

No man thinks more highly than I do of the patriotism, as well as abilities, of the very worthy gentlemen who have just addressed the House. But different men often see the same subject in different lights; and, therefore, I hope that it will not be thought disrespectful to those gentlemen, if, **entertaining** as I do, opinions of a character very opposite to theirs, I shall speak forth my sentiments freely and without reserve. This is no time for ceremony. The question before the House is one of **awful moment** to this country. For my own part I consider it as nothing less than a question of freedom or slavery; and, in proportion to the magnitude of the subject, ought to be the freedom of the debate. It is only in this way that we can hope to arrive at truth, and fulfill the great responsibility which we hold to God and our country. Should I keep back my opinions at such a time, through fear of giving offense, I should consider myself as guilty of treason towards my country, and of an act of disloyalty towards the **Majesty of Heaven**, which I revere above all earthly kings.

entertaining – believing, possessing, holding

awful moment – dire importance

Mr. President, it is natural to men to indulge in the illusions of hope. We are apt to shut our eyes against a painful truth -- and listen to the song of that **siren**, till she transforms us into beasts. Is this the part of wise men, engaged in a great and arduous struggle for liberty? Are we **disposed** to be of the number of those who, having eyes, see not, and having ears, hear not, the things which so nearly concern their **temporal** salvation? For my part, whatever anguish of spirit it may cost, I am willing to know the whole truth; to know the worst and to provide for it.

Majesty of Heaven – God

siren – in Greek myth, a songstress whose singing lured sailors to shipwreck and death

disposed – inclined, willing, receptive

temporal – worldly, non-spiritual, secular

I have but one lamp by which my feet are guided, and that is the lamp of experience. I know of no way of judging of the future but by the past. And judging by the past, I wish to know what there has been in the conduct of the British Ministry for the last ten years to justify those hopes with which gentlemen have been pleased to **solace** themselves and the House? Is it that **insidious** smile with which our petition has been lately received? Trust it not, sir; it will prove a snare to your feet. **Suffer** not yourselves to be betrayed with a kiss. Ask yourself how this gracious reception of our petition **comports** with those war-like preparations which cover our waters and darken our land. Are fleets and armies necessary to a work of love and reconciliation? Have we shown ourselves so unwilling to be reconciled that force must be called in to win back our love? Let us not deceive ourselves, sir. These are the implements of war and subjugation -- the last arguments to which kings resort. I ask gentlemen, sir, what means this **martial** array if its purpose be not to force us to submission? Can gentlemen assign any other possible motive for it? Has Great Britain any enemy, in this quarter of the world, to call for this accumulation of navies and armies? No, sir, she has none. They are meant for us; they can be meant for no other. They are sent over to bind and rivet upon us those chains which the British Ministry have been so long forging.

And what have we to oppose to them? Shall we try argument? Sir, we have been trying that for the last ten years. Have we anything new to offer upon the subject? Nothing. We have held the subject up in every light of which it is capable; but it has been all in vain. Shall we resort to **entreaty** and humble **supplication**? What terms shall we find which have not been already exhausted? Let us not, I beseech you, sir, deceive ourselves longer. Sir, we have done everything that could be done to avert the storm which is now coming on. We have petitioned -- we have **remonstrated** -- we have supplicated -- we have **prostrated** ourselves before the throne, and have implored its **interposition** to arrest the tyrannical hands of the Ministry and Parliament. Our petitions have been **slighted**; our remonstrances have produced additional violence and insult; our supplications have been disregarded; and we have been spurned with contempt from the foot of the throne. In vain, after these things, may we indulge the fond hope of peace and reconciliation.

solace – comfort

insidious – harmful but enticing, deceptive

suffer – permit, allow

comports – correspond, harmonize, agree

martial – military, relating to war

entreaty – plea, appeal

supplication – humble request or prayer

remonstrated – complained, objected

prostrate – lying flat with face on the ground

interposition – intervention, coming between things

slighted – ignored, treated with indifference or insultingly

There is no longer any room for hope. If we wish to be free -- if we mean to preserve **inviolate** those **inestimable** privileges for which we have been so long contending -- if we mean not **basely** to abandon the noble struggle in which we have been so long engaged, and which we have pledged ourselves never to abandon until the glorious object of our contest shall be obtained -- we must fight! -- I repeat it, sir, we must fight; an appeal to arms and to the God of Hosts is all that is left us!

They tell us, sir, that we are weak -- unable to cope with so **formidable** an adversary. But when shall we be stronger? Will it be the next week or the next year? Will it be when we are totally disarmed, and when a British guard shall be stationed in every house? Shall we gather strength by **irresolution** and inaction? Shall we acquire the means of effectual resistance by lying **supinely** on our backs and hugging the delusive phantom of hope, until our enemy shall have bound us hand and foot? Sir, we are not weak, if we make a proper use of those forces which the God of nature hath placed in our power. Three millions of people armed in the holy cause of liberty, and in such a country as that which we possess, are invincible by any force which our enemy can send against us.

Besides, sir, we shall not fight our battles alone. There is a just God who presides over the destinies of nations, and who will raise up friends to fight our battles for us. The battle, sir, is not to the strong alone; it is to the **vigilant**, the active, the brave. Besides, sir, we have no **election**. If we were base enough to desire it, it is now too late to retire from the contest. There is no retreat but in submission and slavery! Our chains are forged! Their clanking may be heard on the plains of Boston! The war is inevitable -- and let it come! I repeat it, sir, let it come!

It is vain, sir, to **extenuate** the matter. Gentlemen may cry, peace, peace -- but there is no peace. The war is actually begun! The next gale that sweeps from the north will bring to our ears the clash of resounding arms! Our **brethren** are already in the field! Why stand we here idle? What is it that gentlemen wish? What would they have? Is life so dear, or

inviolate – sacred, intact, free from injury

inestimable – too great to calculate

basely – ignoble, lacking honor or morality

formidable – difficult to overcome, inspiring fear or dread

irresolution – hesitancy, indecisiveness

supinely – lying on the back, showing passivity

vigilant – alertly watchful, especially to avoid danger

election – choice

extenuate – draw out, try to lessen or represent as less serious

brethren – fellow members, brothers, kinsmen

peace so sweet, as to be purchased at the price of chains and slavery? Forbid it, Almighty God! I know not what course others may take; but as for me, give me liberty, or give me death!

Liberty or Death

1. Patrick Henry is reacting to recent British:
   A. laws
   B. armament
   C. taxation

2. The speaker directs his anger chiefly to England's:
   A. King
   B. Parliament
   C. soldiers of occupation

3. Henry believes that in a conflict with England, America may in fact be:
   A. victorious
   B. outgunned
   C. united

4. Henry regards the colonies' greatest potential ally as:
   A. France
   B. sympathetic Englishmen
   C. God

5. Henry places the highest value on:
   A. independence
   B. freedom
   C. peaceful coexistence

6. The word *slight* as used (¶ 4) most nearly relates to:
   A. a warship
   B. a trifle
   C. an insult

7. Henry claims that these may be heard "on the plains of Boston":
   A. chains
   B. the shouts of Patriots
   C. the weeping of widows

8. Henry says that colonial resistance so far has depended on:
   A. prayer
   B. argument
   C. threats

9. Henry's speech is being delivered in:
   A. Boston
   B. Philadelphia
   C. Richmond

10. The colonies are said to have in their conflict with the motherland the support of:
   A. the populace
   B. foreign allies
   C. destiny

Lincoln's Second Inaugural Address March 1865

At a time when victory over the secessionists in the American Civil War was within days and slavery was near an end, Lincoln did not speak triumphantly.

Fellow-countrymen: At this second appearing to take the oath of the presidential office, there is less occasion for an extended address than there was at the first. Then a statement, somewhat in detail, of a course to be pursued, seemed fitting and proper. Now, at the expiration of four years, during which public declarations have been constantly called forth on every point and phase of the **great contest** which still absorbs the attention and **engrosses** the energies of the nation, little that is new could be presented. The progress of our arms, upon which all else chiefly depends, is as well known to the public as to myself; and it is, I trust, reasonably satisfactory and encouraging to all. With high hope for the future, no prediction in regard to it is ventured.

On the occasion corresponding to this four years ago, all thoughts were anxiously directed to an **impending** civil war. All dreaded it—all sought to avert it. While the inaugural address was being delivered from this place, devoted altogether to saving the Union without war, **insurgent** agents were in the city seeking to destroy it without war—seeking to dissolve the Union, and divide effects, by negotiation. Both parties **deprecated** war; but one of them would make war rather than let the nation survive; and the other would accept war rather than let it perish. And the war came.

One-eighth of the whole population were colored slaves, not distributed generally over the Union, but localized in the Southern part of it. These slaves constituted a peculiar and powerful interest. All knew that this interest was, somehow, the cause of the war. To strengthen, **perpetuate**, and extend this interest was the object for which the insurgents would rend the Union, even by war; while the government claimed no right to do more than to restrict the territorial enlargement of it. Neither party expected for the war the magnitude or the duration which it has already attained. Neither anticipated that the cause of the conflict might cease with, or even before, the

inauguration – commencement, formal induction into office

great contest – the American Civil War

engross – occupy completely, absorb

impending – about to occur, looming

insurgent – rebellious, revolting against authority

deprecated – deplore, express disapproval of

perpetuate – cause to last or continue

conflict itself should cease. Each looked for an easier triumph, and a result less fundamental and **astounding**. Both read the same Bible, and pray to the same God; and each **invokes** his aid against the other. It may seem strange that any men should dare to ask a just God's assistance in wringing their bread from the sweat of other men's faces; but let us judge not, that we be not judged. The prayers of both could not be answered—that of neither has been answered fully. The Almighty has his own purposes. "Woe unto the world because of offenses! for it must needs be that offenses come; but woe to that man by whom the offense cometh." If we shall suppose that American slavery is one of those offenses which, in the **providence** of God, must needs come, but which, having continued through his appointed time, he now wills to remove, and that he gives to both North and South this terrible war, as the woe due to those by whom the offense came, shall we **discern** therein any departure from those divine attributes which the believers in a living God always ascribe to him? Fondly do we hope—**fervently** do we pray—that this mighty **scourge** of war may speedily pass away. Yet, if God wills that it continue until all the wealth piled by the **bondman**'s two hundred and fifty years of **unrequited** toil shall be sunk, and until every drop of blood drawn with the lash shall be paid by another drawn with the sword, as was said three thousand years ago, so still it must be said, "The judgments of the Lord are true and righteous altogether."

With **malice** toward none; with **charity** for all; with firmness in the right, as God gives us to see the right, let us strive on to finish the work we are in; to bind up the nation's wounds; to care for him who shall have borne the battle, and for his widow, and his orphan—to do all which may achieve and cherish a just and lasting peace among ourselves, and with all nations.

astounding – astonishing, amazing

invoke – appeal, call on

providence – divine intervention, guidance or care, providing

discern – detect, see, discriminate

fervent – showing great feeling, zealous

scourge – whip, means of inflicting suffering

bondsman – slave

unrequited – not returned in kind or reciprocated

malice – desire to cause pain, injury, or distress to another

charity – good will, benevolence

Lincoln's Second Inaugural

1. An "*inaugural*" is a speech made when:
    A. a war is undertaken
    B. a term of office begins
    C. a prediction is offered

2. Lincoln suggests that a Northern victory is:
    A. inevitable
    B. uncertain
    C. accomplished

3. Four years earlier, Lincoln says the South believed war:
    A. was essentially underway
    B. could be averted
    C. was probably unavoidable

4. When the war began, both sides believed it would result in:
    A. a quick end
    B. a compromise on slavery
    C. sectional hatred

5. Lincoln implies that God has supported:
    A. the North
    B. the South
    C. neither side

6. Lincoln's stance toward the secessionists is:
    A. to re-educate
    B. to bury the past
    C. to give aid

7. The word "*impending*" as used here (¶ 2) most nearly means:
    A. starting soon
    B. inevitable
    C. touching

8. Lincoln says the cause of the war in the government's view was:
    A. civil rights
    B. states' rights
    C. slavery's expansion

9. Lincoln says his main hope now is for:
    A. brotherhood
    B. peace
    C. veterans' care

10. Frequent reference is made to:
    A. the Founding Fathers
    B. the Founding documents
    C. the Bible

The Little Match-Seller
Hans Christian Anderson 1835

Hans Christian Andersen – Danish author best remembered for his fairy tales

It was terribly cold and nearly dark on the last evening of the old year, and the snow was falling fast. In the cold and the darkness, a poor little girl, with bare head and naked feet, roamed through the streets. It is true she had on a pair of slippers when she left home, but they were not of much use.

They were very large, so large, indeed, that they had belonged to her mother, and the poor little creature had lost them in running across the street to avoid two carriages that were rolling along at a terrible rate. One of the slippers she could not find, and a boy seized upon the other and ran away with it, saying that he could use it as a cradle, when he had children of his own. So the little girl went on with her little naked feet, which were quite red and blue with the cold. In an old apron she carried a number of matches, and had a bundle of them in her hands. No one had bought anything of her the whole day, nor had any one given her even a penny.

Shivering with cold and hunger, she crept along; poor little child, she looked the picture of misery. The snowflakes fell on her long, fair hair, which hung in curls on her shoulders, but she regarded them not.

Lights were shining from every window, and there was a savory smell of roast goose, for it was New-year's eve- yes, she remembered that. In a corner, between two houses, one of which projected beyond the other, she sank down and huddled herself together. She had drawn her little feet under her, but she could not keep off the cold; and she dared not go home, for she had sold no matches, and could not take home even a penny of money. Her father would certainly beat her; besides, it was almost as cold at home as here, for they had only the roof to cover them, through which the wind howled, although the largest holes had been stopped up with straw and rags. Her little hands were almost frozen with the cold. Ah! perhaps a burning match might be some good, if she could draw it from the bundle and strike it against the wall, just to warm her fingers. She drew one out -"scratch!" how it sputtered as it burnt! It gave a warm, bright light, like a little candle, as she held her hand over it. It was really a wonderful light. It seemed to the little girl that she was sitting by a large iron stove, with polished brass feet and a brass ornament. How the fire burned! and seemed so beautifully warm that the child stretched out her feet as if to warm them, when, lo! the flame of the match went out, the stove vanished, and she had only the remains of the half-burnt match in her hand.

She rubbed another match on the wall. It burst into a flame, and where its light fell upon the wall it became as transparent as a veil, and she could see into the room. The table was covered with a snowy white table-cloth, on which stood a splendid dinner service, and a steaming roast goose, stuffed with apples and dried plums. And what was still more wonderful, the goose jumped down from the dish and waddled across the floor, with a knife and fork in its breast, to the little girl. Then the match went out, and there remained nothing but the thick, damp, cold wall before her.

She lighted another match, and then she found herself sitting under a beautiful Christmas-tree. It was larger and more beautifully decorated than the one which she had seen through the glass door at the rich merchant's. Thousands of **tapers** were burning upon the green branches, and colored pictures, like those she had seen in the show-windows, looked down upon it all. The little one stretched out her hand towards them, and the match went out.

taper – a slender candle

The Christmas lights rose higher and higher, till they looked to her like the stars in the sky. Then she saw a star fall, leaving behind it a bright streak of fire. "Someone is dying," thought the little girl, for her old grandmother, the only one who had ever loved her, and who was now dead, had told her that when a star falls, a soul was going up to God.

She again rubbed a match on the wall, and the light shone round her; in the brightness stood her old grandmother, clear and shining, yet mild and loving in her appearance.

"Grandmother," cried the little one, "O take me with you; I know you will go away when the match burns out; you will vanish like the warm stove, the roast goose, and the large,

111

glorious Christmas-tree." And she made haste to light the whole bundle of matches, for she wished to keep her grandmother there. And the matches glowed with a light that was brighter than the noon-day, and her grandmother had never appeared so large or so beautiful. She took the little girl in her arms, and they both flew upwards in brightness and joy far above the earth, where there was neither cold nor hunger nor pain, for they were with God.

In the dawn of morning there lay the poor little one, with pale cheeks and smiling mouth, leaning against the wall; she had been frozen to death on the last evening of the year; and the New-year's sun rose and shone upon a little corpse! The child still sat, in the stiffness of death, holding the matches in her hand, one bundle of which was burnt. "She tried to warm herself," said some. No one imagined what beautiful things she had seen, nor into what glory she had entered with her grandmother, on New-year's day.

The Little Match-Seller

1. The little girl has lost her:
   A. slippers
   B. way
   C. mother

2. The story takes place on:
   A. Christmas Eve
   B. Christmas
   C. New Year's Eve

3. The girl attempts to keep warm with:
   A. chimney smoke
   B. a threadbare coat
   C. a small flame

4. It is implied that the girl expires from:
   A. delusion
   B. hunger
   C. freezing

5. At the story's end the girl feels:
   A. joyous
   B. desperate
   C. abandoned

6. The word "taper" as used in the passage relates to the girl's:
   A. food
   B. illumination
   C. figure

7. The story might best be classified as:
   A. a religious fable
   B. a fairy tale
   C. an allegory

8. The girl decides not to go home because she had:
   A. lost her shoes
   B. burned up all her matches
   C. earned no money

9. A passing boy steals the girl's:
   A. scarf
   B. slipper
   C. gloves

10. Through a window, the girl sees:
    A. a Christmas tree
    B. her home fireplace
    C. her grandmother

The Mass Of Shadows
Anatole France 1921

This tale the **sacristan** of the church of St. Eulalie at **Neuville d'Aumont** told me, as we sat under the **arbor** of the White Horse, one fine summer evening, drinking a bottle of old wine to the health of the dead man, now very much at his ease, whom that very morning he had borne to the grave with full honors, beneath a **pall** powdered with smart silver tears.

"My poor father who is dead" (it is the sacristan who is speaking,) "was in his lifetime a grave-digger. He was of an agreeable disposition, the result, no doubt, of the **calling** he followed, for it has often been pointed out that people who work in cemeteries are of a **jovial turn**. Death has no terrors for them; they never give it a thought. I, for instance, monsieur, enter a cemetery at night as little perturbed as though it were the arbor of the White Horse. And if by chance I meet with a ghost, I don't disturb myself in the least about it, for I reflect that he may just as likely have business of his own to attend to as I. I know the habits of the dead, and I know their character. Indeed, so far as that goes, I know things of which the priests themselves are ignorant. If I were to tell you all I have seen, you would be astounded. But a still tongue makes a wise head, and my father, who, all the same, delighted in **spinning a yarn**, did not disclose a twentieth part of what he knew. To make up for this he often repeated the same stories, and to my knowledge he told the story of Catherine Fontaine at least a hundred times.

"Catherine Fontaine was an old maid whom he well remembered having seen when he was a mere child. I should not be surprised if there were still, perhaps, three old fellows in the district who could remember having heard folks speak of her, for she was very well known and of excellent reputation, though poor enough. She lived at the corner of the **Rue** aux Nonnes, in the turret which is still to be seen there, and which formed part of an old half-ruined mansion looking on to the garden of the Ursuline nuns. On that turret can still be traced certain figures and half-obliterated inscriptions. The late **curé** of St. Eulalie, Monsieur Levasseur, asserted that

Anatole France – French poet, journalist, and novelist

sacristan – person in charge of sacred church vessels, vestments; taking care of minor church duties; sexton

Neuville d'Aumont – northern France town

arbor – a leafy, shady recess formed by tree branches

pall – coffin or a cloth covering it

calling – profession

jovial – jolly, convivial, good-humored, of good cheer

turn – character, inclination, bent

spin a yarn – tell a tale

rue – street (Fr.)

curé – parish priest

114

there are the words in Latin, Love is stronger than death, 'which is to be understood,' so he would add, 'of divine love.'

"Catherine Fontaine lived by herself in this tiny apartment. She was a lace-maker. You know, of course, that the lace made in our part of the world was formerly held in high esteem. No one knew anything of her relatives or friends. It was reported that when she was eighteen years of age she had loved the young **Chevalier** d'Aumont-Cléry, and had been secretly **affianced** to him. But decent folk didn't believe a word of it, and said it was nothing but a tale concocted because Catherine Fontaine's **demeanor** was that of a lady rather than that of a working woman, and because, moreover, she possessed beneath her white locks the remains of great beauty. Her expression was sorrowful, and on one finger she wore one of those rings fashioned by the goldsmith into the semblance of two tiny hands clasped together. In former days folks were accustomed to exchange such rings at their **betrothal** ceremony. I am sure you know the sort of thing I mean.

"Catherine Fontaine lived a saintly life. She spent a great deal of time in churches, and every morning, whatever might be the weather, she went to assist at the six o'clock Mass at St. Eulalie.

"Now one December night, whilst she was in her little chamber, she was awakened by the sound of bells, and nothing doubting that they were ringing for the first Mass, the pious woman dressed herself, and came downstairs and out into the street. The night was so **obscure** that not even the walls of the houses were visible, and not a ray of light shone from the murky sky. And such was the silence amid this black darkness, that there was not even the sound of a distant dog barking, and a feeling of **aloofness** from every living creature was perceptible. But Catherine Fontaine knew well every single stone she stepped on, and, as she could have found her way to the church with her eyes shut, she reached without difficulty the corner of the Rue aux Nonnes and the Rue de la Paroisse, where the timbered house stands with the **tree of Jesse** carved on one of its massive beams. When she reached this spot she perceived that the church doors were open, and

chevalier – knight, cavalier

affianced – engaged to marry

demeanor – behavior, appearance

betrothal – engagement, promise to marry

obscure – dark

aloofness – emotional reserve or distance

tree of Jesse – a branching artistic depiction of the ancestors of Christ, beginning with Jesse, the father of king David

that a great light was streaming out from the wax **tapers**. She resumed her journey, and when she had passed through the porch she found herself in the midst of a vast congregation which entirely filled the church. But she did not recognize any of the worshipers and was surprised to observe that all of these people were dressed in velvets and **brocades** with feathers in their hats, and that they wore swords in the fashion of days gone by. Here were gentlemen who carried tall canes with gold knobs, and ladies with lace caps fastened with **coronet**-shaped combs. Chevaliers of the Order of St. Louis extended their hands to these ladies, who concealed behind their fans **painted** faces, of which only the powdered brow and the patch at the corner of the eye were visible! All of them proceeded to take their places without the slightest sound, and as they moved neither the sound of their footsteps on the pavement, nor the rustle of their garments could be heard. The lower places were filled with a crowd of young artisans in brown jackets, **dimity** breeches, and blue stockings, with their arms round the waists of pretty blushing girls who lowered their eyes. Near the holy water **stoups** peasant women, in scarlet petticoats and laced **bodices**, sat upon the ground as immovable as domestic animals, whilst young lads, standing up behind them, stared out from wide-open eyes and twirled their hats round and round on their fingers, and all these sorrowful **countenances** centred irremovably on one and the same thought, at once sweet and sorrowful. On her knees, in her accustomed place, Catherine Fontaine saw the priest advance toward the altar, preceded by two servers. She recognized neither priest nor clerks. The Mass began. It was a silent Mass, during which neither the sound of the moving lips nor the tinkle of the bell was audible. Catherine Fontaine felt that she was under the observation and the influence also of her mysterious neighbor, and when, scarcely turning her head, she stole a glance at him, she recognized the young Chevalier d'Aumont-Cléry, who had once loved her, and who had been dead for five and forty years. She recognized him by a small mark which he had over the left ear, and above all by the shadow which his long black eyelashes cast upon his cheeks. He was dressed in his hunting clothes, scarlet with gold lace, the very clothes he wore that day when he met her in St. Leonard's

tapers – slender candles

brocade – heavy fabric interwoven with a rich, raised design

coronet – small crown, ornamental headband

painted – cosmetically made up

dimity – sheer corded cotton fabric

stoup – basin for holy water at a church entrance

bodice – upper part of a woman's dress, sleeveless outer garment covering the waist and bust

countenances – faces

Wood, begged of her a drink, and stole a kiss. He had preserved his youth and good looks. When he smiled, he still displayed magnificent teeth. Catherine said to him in an undertone:

"'Monseigneur, you who were my friend, and to whom in days gone by I gave all that a girl holds most dear, may God keep you in His grace! O, that He would at length inspire me with regret for the sin I committed in yielding to you; for it is a fact that, though my hair is white and I approach my end, I have not yet repented of having loved you. But, dear dead friend and noble **seigneur**, tell me, who are these folk, **habited** after the antique fashion, who are here assisting at this silent Mass?'

seigneur – feudal lord

habited – dressed, clothed

"The Chevalier d'Aumont-Cléry replied in a voice feebler than a breath, but none the less crystal clear:

"'Catherine, these men and women are souls from **purgatory** who have grieved God by sinning as we ourselves sinned through love of the creature, but who are not on that account cast off by God, inasmuch as their sin, like ours, was not deliberate.

purgatory – in Catholic Church doctrine, is an intermediate state after physical death in which those destined for heaven "undergo purification"

"'Whilst separated from those whom they loved upon earth, they are purified in the cleansing fires of purgatory, they suffer the pangs of absence, which is for them the most cruel of tortures. They are so unhappy that an angel from heaven takes pity upon their love-torment. By the permission of the Most High, for one hour in the night, he reunites each year lover to loved in their parish church, where they are permitted to assist at the Mass of Shadows, hand clasped in hand. These are the facts. If it has been granted to me to see thee before thy death, Catherine, it is a **boon** which is bestowed by God's special permission.'

boon – benefit

"And Catherine Fontaine answered him:

"'I would die gladly enough, dear, dead lord, if I might recover the beauty that was mine when I gave you to drink in the forest.'

117

"Whilst they thus conversed under their breath, a very old **canon** was taking the collection and proffering to the worshipers a great copper dish, wherein they let fall, each in his turn, ancient coins which have long since ceased to pass current: écus of six livres, florins, ducats and ducatoons, jacobuses and rose-nobles, and the pieces fell silently into the dish. When at length it was placed before the Chevalier, he dropped into it a **louis** made no more sound than had the other pieces of gold and silver.

"Then the old canon stopped before Catherine Fontaine, who fumbled in her pocket without being able to find a **farthing**. Then, being unwilling to allow the dish to pass without an offering from herself, she slipped from her finger the ring which the Chevalier had given her the day before his death, and cast it into the copper bowl. As the golden ring fell, a sound like the heavy clang of a bell rang out, and on the stroke of this reverberation the Chevalier, the canon, the celebrant, the servers, the ladies and their cavaliers, the whole assembly vanished utterly; the candles **guttered** out, and Catherine Fontaine was left alone in the darkness."

Having concluded his narrative after this fashion, the sacristan drank a long draught of wine, remained pensive for a moment, and then resumed his talk in these words:

"I have told you this tale exactly as my father has told it to me over and over again, and I believe that it is authentic, because it agrees in all respects with what I have observed of the manners and customs peculiar to those who have passed away. I have associated a good deal with the dead ever since my childhood, and I know that they are accustomed to return to what they have loved.

"It is on this account that the **miserly** dead wander at night in the neighborhood of the treasures they conceal during their life time. They keep a strict watch over their gold; but the trouble they give themselves, far from being of service to them, turns to their disadvantage; and it is not a rare thing at all to come upon money buried in the ground on digging in a place haunted by a ghost. In the same way deceased husbands

canon – staff clergyman

louis – a former French gold coin worth 20 francs

farthing – former monetary unit equal to 1/4 of a penny

gutter – burn sputteringly

miserly – giving or sharing as little as possible

118

come by night to harass their wives who have made a second matrimonial venture, and I could easily name several who have kept a better watch over their wives since death than they ever did while living.

"That sort of thing is blameworthy, for in all fairness the dead have no business to stir up jealousies. Still I do but tell you what I have observed myself. It is a matter to take into account if one marries a widow. Besides, the tale I have told you is **vouchsafed** for in the manner following:

"The morning after that extraordinary night Catherine Fontaine was discovered dead in her chamber. And the **beadle** attached to St. Eulalie found in the copper bowl used for the collection a gold ring with two clasped hands. Besides, I'm not the kind of man to make jokes. Suppose we order another bottle of wine?"

vouchsafed – granted, bestowed, promised

beadle – church usher or official with minor duties

The Mass of Shadows

1. The story was first told by a:
   A. grave-digger
   B. gentleman
   C. church official

2. The story can be said to contain what kind of events:
   A. historical
   B. nightmarish
   C. paranormal

3. Catherine performs an act in the church that shows:
   A. sacrifice
   B. obedience
   C. distrust

4. Catherine was at one time:
   A. engaged
   B. widowed
   C. left at the altar

5. Catherine says she would gladly die if this could be restored to her:
   A. her betrothed
   B. her beauty
   C. her former home life

6. The word "*canon*" (p. 118) in the passage most nearly means:
   A. a round of song
   B. an armament
   C. a churchman

7. The Chevalier has been dead for:
   A. for one hour
   B. for one day
   C. for 45 years

8. The narrator enumerates the several coins taken up in the church collection to show:
   A. the parish's fair expectations
   B. the age of the story
   C. Catherine's poverty

9. Those souls in purgatory suffer this "most cruel of tortures":
   A. the wages of sin
   B. the pains of absence
   C. removal from the angels

10. The story takes place among gathered inhabitants of a French:
    A. church
    B. castle
    C. cemetery

Of Studies
Francis Bacon 1625

Studies serve for delight, for **ornament**, and for ability. Their chief use for delight is in privateness and retiring; for ornament, is in discourse; and for ability, is in the judgment and disposition of business. For expert men can execute, and perhaps judge of particulars, one by one; but the general counsels, and the plots and **marshalling** of affairs, come best from those that are learned. To spend too much time in studies is **sloth**; to use them too much for ornament, is affectation; to make judgment wholly by their rules, is the **humor** of a scholar. They perfect nature, and are perfected by experience: for natural abilities are like natural plants, that need pruning, by study; and studies themselves do give forth directions too much at large, except they be bounded in by experience. Crafty men condemn studies, simple men admire them, and wise men use them; for they teach not their own use; but that is a wisdom without them, and above them, won by observation. Read not to contradict and **confute**; nor to believe and take for granted; nor to find talk and discourse; but to weigh and consider. Some books are to be tasted, others to be swallowed, and some few to be chewed and digested; that is, some books are to be read only in parts; others to be read, but not curiously; and some few to be read wholly, and with diligence and attention. Some books also may be read by **deputy**, and extracts made of them by others; but that would be only in the less important arguments, and the **meaner** sort of books, else distilled books are like common distilled waters, flashy things. Reading maketh a full man; conference a ready man; and writing an exact man. And therefore, if a man write little, he had need have a great memory; if he confer little, he had need have a present **wit**: and if he read little, he had need have much cunning, to seem to know that he doth not. Histories make men wise; poets witty; the mathematics subtle; **natural philosophy** deep; moral grave; logic and rhetoric able to contend. *Abeunt studia in mores* [Studies pass into and influence manners]. Nay, there is no stone or impediment in the wit but may be wrought out by fit studies; like as diseases of the body may have appropriate exercises. Bowling is good for the stone and

Francis Bacon – statesman, philosopher, essayist, scientist – and a contemporary of William Shakespeare

ornament – eloquence, powerful, colorful, or persuasive use of language

marshalling – arranging

sloth – laziness, inactivity

humor – disposition, behavior, inclination

confute – prove false or invalid, disprove

deputy – an appointed substitute

meaner – inferior in quality

wit – intelligence, understanding, shrewdness

natural philosophy – philosophical study of nature and the physical universe before the advent of science

reins; shooting for the lungs and breast; gentle walking for the stomach; riding for the head; and the like. So if a man's wit be wandering, let him study the mathematics; for in demonstrations, if his wit be called away never so little, he must begin again. If his wit be not apt to distinguish or find differences, let him study the **Schoolmen**; for they are *cymini sectores* [splitters of hairs]. If he be not apt to **beat over** matters, and to call up one thing to prove and illustrate another, let him study the lawyers' cases. So every defect of the mind may have a special **receipt**.

Schoolmen – medieval university scholars, scholastics

beat over – mull over, belabor

receipt – reception, answer, response

Of Studies

1. Spending large amounts of time in studies is said to indicate:
   - A. self-absorption
   - B. inactivity
   - C. scholarly

2. Studies for activity are said to be useful for:
   - A. debating
   - B. business
   - C. teaching

3. Bacon likens studies to plants because they involve:
   - A. growth
   - B. light
   - C. pruning

4. Writing is said to produce a man who is:
   - A. exact
   - B. cunning
   - C. ready

5. Bacon claims that this particular exercise is good for the head:
   - A. shooting
   - B. riding
   - C. walking

6. "If a man write little, he had need of":
   - A. conference
   - B. memory
   - C. wit

7. The meaning of "*humor*" as referred to here is:
   - A. mood
   - B. joviality
   - C. tendency

8. The company of scholarly *hair splitters* may promote:
   - A. sharp debate
   - B. finding differences
   - C. impatience

9. These sorts of men condemn studies:
   - A. crafty
   - B. politicians
   - C. simpletons

10. This piece of prose is best classified as:
   - A. a scholarly lecture
   - B. a legal definition
   - C. an essay

The Open Window
H. H. Munro, pen name Saki 1914

"My aunt will come down very soon, Mr. Nuttel," said a very calm young lady of fifteen years of age; "meanwhile you must try to **bear** my company."

Framton Nuttel tried to say something which would please the niece now present, without annoying the aunt that was about to come. He was supposed to be going through a cure for his nerves; but he doubted whether these polite visits to a number of total strangers would help much.

"I know how it will be," his sister had said when he was preparing to go away into the country; "you will lose yourself down there and not speak to a **living soul**, and your nerves will be worse than ever through loneliness. I shall just give you letters of introduction to all the people I know there. Some of them, as far as I can remember, were quite nice."

Framton wondered whether Mrs. Sappleton, the lady to whom he was bringing one of the **letters of introduction**, was one of the nice ones.

"Do you know many of the people round here?" asked the niece, when she thought that they had sat long enough in silence.

"Hardly one," said Framton. "My sister was staying here, you know, about four years ago, and she gave me letters of introduction to some of the people here."

He made the last statement in a sad voice.

"Then you know almost nothing about my aunt?" continued the calm young lady.

"Only her name and address," Framton admitted. He was wondering whether Mrs. Sappleton was married; perhaps she had been married and her husband was dead. But there was something of a man in the room.

H. H. Munro – English writer, considered a master of witty, often macabre short stories

bear – put up with, tolerate

living soul – person, human being

letter of introduction – a letter given from one person to another, as an introduction to a third party

124

"Her great sorrow came just three years ago," said the child. "That would be after your sister's time."

"Her sorrow?" asked Framton. Somehow, in this restful country place, sorrows seemed far away.

"You may wonder why we keep that window wide open on an October afternoon," said the niece, pointing to a long window that opened like a door on to the grass outside.

"It is quite warm for the time of the year," said Framton; "but has that window got anything to do with your aunt's sorrow?"

"Out through that window, exactly three years ago, her husband and her two young brothers went off for their day's shooting. They never came back. In crossing the country to the shooting-ground, they were all three swallowed in a **bog**. It had been that terrible wet summer, you know, and places that were safe in other years became suddenly dangerous. Their bodies were never found. That was the worst part of it." Here the child's voice lost its calm sound and became almost human. "Poor aunt always thinks that they will come back some day, they and the little brown dog that was lost with them, and walk in at that window just as they used to do. That is why the window is kept open every evening till it is quite dark. Poor dear aunt, she has often told me how they went out, her husband with his white coat over his arm, and Ronnie, her youngest brother, singing a song, as he always did to annoy her, because she said it affected her nerves. Do you know, sometimes on quiet evenings like this, I almost get a strange feeling that they will all walk in through the window-----"

bog – wet, muddy ground too soft to support a heavy body

She stopped and trembled. It was a relief to Framton when the aunt came busily into the room and apologized for being late.

"I hope Vera has been amusing you?" she said.

"She has been very interesting," said Framton.

125

"I hope you don't mind the open window," said Mrs. Sappleton brightly; "my husband and brothers will be home soon from shooting, and they always come in this way. They've been shooting birds to-day near the bog, so they'll make my poor carpets dirty. All you men do that sort of thing, don't you?"

She talked on cheerfully about the shooting and the scarcity of birds, and the hopes of shooting in the winter. To Framton it was all quite terrible. He made a great effort, which was only partly successful, to turn the talk on to a more cheerful subject. He was conscious that his hostess was giving him only a part of her attention, and her eyes were frequently looking past him to the open window and the grass beyond. It was certainly unfortunate that he should have paid his visit on this sorrowful day.

"The doctors agree in ordering me complete rest, no excitement and no bodily exercise," said Framton, who had the common idea that total strangers want to know the least detail of one's illnesses, their cause and cure. "On the matter of food, they are not so much in agreement," he continued.

"No?" said Mrs. Sappleton in a tired voice. Then she suddenly brightened into attention - but not to what Framton was saying.

"Here they are at last!" she cried; "just in time for tea, and don't they look as if they were muddy up to the eyes!"

Framton trembled slightly and turned towards the niece with a look intended to show sympathetic understanding.

The child was looking out through the open window with fear in her eyes. With a shock Framton turned round in his seat and looked in the same direction.

In the increasing darkness three figures were walking across the grass towards the window; they all carried guns under their arms, and one of them had also a white coat hung over his shoulders. A tired brown dog kept close at their heels.

Noiselessly they drew near to the house, and then a young voice started to sing in the darkness.

Framton wildly seized his hat and **stick**; he ran out through the front door and through the gate. He nearly ran into a man on a bicycle.

stick – cane, walking stick

"Here we are, my dear," said the bearer of the white coat, coming in through the window; "fairly muddy, but most of it's dry. Who was that who ran out as we came up?"

"A most extraordinary man, a Mr. Nuttel," said Mrs. Sappleton; "he could only talk about his illnesses, and ran off without a word of good-bye or apology when you arrived. One would think he had seen a ghost."

"I expect it was the dog," said the niece calmly; "he told me he had a terrible fear of dogs. He was once hunted into a graveyard somewhere in India by a lot of wild dogs, and had to spend the night in a newly-dug grave with the creatures just above him. Enough to make anyone lose their nerve."

She was very clever at making up stories quickly.

The Open Window

1. Nuttel's letters of introduction are from:
   A. Mrs. Sappleton
   B. His sister
   C. His boss

2. Nuttel has gone to the country to:
   A. hunt
   B. visit acquaintances
   C. improve his health

3. Mrs. Sappleton and the others in the house are to Nuttel:
   A. his relatives
   B. old friends
   C. strangers

4. The niece is most accurately described as a:
   A. storyteller
   B. tomboy
   C. spoiled brat

5. Nuttel flees the scene because of:
   A. fright
   B. the dog
   C. sudden illness

6. The word "*bog*" as used in the passage most nearly means:
   A. pit
   B. swamp
   C. buddy

7. The niece, Vera, is most accurately characterized as a:
   A. storyteller
   B. tomboy
   C. spirit

8. Nuttle flees the scene because he fears:
   A. ghosts
   B. dogs
   C. the niece

9. The niece looks "*through the window with fear in her eyes*" because she worries about:
   A. her aunt's anger
   B. being caught in a lie
   C. Nuttel's being panicked

10. According to Vera, three men disappeared along with a:
    A. guide
    B. dog
    C. gamekeeper

The Oval Portrait
Edgar Allan Poe 1842

The **chateau** into which my **valet** had ventured to make forcible entrance, rather than permit me, in my desperately wounded condition, to pass a night in the open air, was one of those piles of commingled gloom and grandeur which have so long frowned among the **Appennines**, not less in fact than in the fancy of **Mrs. Radcliffe**. To all appearance it had been temporarily and very lately abandoned. We established ourselves in one of the smallest and least **sumptuously** furnished apartments. It lay in a remote turret of the building. Its decorations were rich, yet tattered and antique. Its walls were hung with tapestry and bedecked with **manifold** and multiform **armorial** trophies, together with an unusually great number of very spirited modern paintings in frames of rich golden **arabesque**. In these paintings, which **depended** from the walls not only in their main surfaces, but in very many nooks which the bizarre architecture of the chateau rendered necessary- in these paintings my **incipient** delirium, perhaps, had caused me to take deep interest; so that I bade Pedro to close the heavy shutters of the room- since it was already night- to light the tongues of a tall candelabrum which stood by the head of my bed- and to throw open far and wide the fringed curtains of black velvet which enveloped the bed itself. I wished all this done that I might resign myself, if not to sleep, at least alternately to the contemplation of these pictures, and the perusal of a small volume which had been found upon the pillow, and which purported to criticise and describe them.

Long - long I read - and devoutly, devotedly I gazed. Rapidly and gloriously the hours flew by and the deep midnight came. The position of the candelabrum displeased me, and outreaching my hand with difficulty, rather than disturb my slumbering valet, I placed it so as to throw its rays more fully upon the book.

But the action produced an effect altogether unanticipated. The rays of the numerous candles (for there were many) now fell within a niche of the room which had **hitherto** been thrown into deep shade by one of the bed-posts. I thus saw in

Edgar Allan Poe – American writer of mysterious, macabre short stories, inventor of detective fiction

château – manor house, French castle

valet – a gentleman's male attendant/servant

Appennines – Italian mountain range

Mrs. Radcliffe – author of Gothic novels dealing with the supernatural

sumptuous – extremely costly, lavish, luxurious

manifold – numerous

armorial – relating to a coat of arms

arabesque – intricate or elaborate pattern/design

depended – hung

incipient – beginning to exist

hitherto – up until now

vivid light a picture all unnoticed before. It was the portrait of a young girl just ripening into womanhood. I glanced at the painting hurriedly, and then closed my eyes. Why I did this was not at first apparent even to my own perception. But while my lids remained thus shut, I ran over in my mind my reason for so shutting them. It was an impulsive movement to gain time for thought- to make sure that my vision had not deceived me- to calm and subdue my fancy for a more sober and more certain gaze. In a very few moments I again looked fixedly at the painting.

That I now saw aright I could not and would not doubt; for the first flashing of the candles upon that canvas had seemed to **dissipate** the dreamy **stupor** which was **stealing over** my senses, and to startle me at once into waking life.

The portrait, I have already said, was that of a young girl. It was a mere head and shoulders, done in what is technically termed a **vignette** manner; much in the style of the favorite heads of **Sully**. The arms, the bosom, and even the ends of the radiant hair melted imperceptibly into the vague yet deep shadow which formed the back-ground of the whole. The frame was oval, richly gilded and **filigreed** in **Moresque**. As a thing of art nothing could be more admirable than the painting itself. But it could have been neither the execution of the work, nor the immortal beauty of the **countenance**, which had so suddenly and so vehemently moved me. Least of all, could it have been that my **fancy**, shaken from its half slumber, had mistaken the head for that of a living person. I saw at once that the peculiarities of the design, of the vignetting, and of the frame, must have instantly dispelled such idea- must have prevented even its momentary entertainment. Thinking earnestly upon these points, I remained, for an hour perhaps, half sitting, half reclining, with my vision riveted upon the portrait. At length, satisfied with the true secret of its effect, I fell back within the bed. I had found the spell of the picture in an absolute life-likeliness of expression, which, at first startling, finally **confounded**, subdued, and appalled me. With deep and reverent awe I replaced the candelabrum in its former position. The cause of my deep **agitation** being thus shut from view, I sought

dissipate – gradually vanish, scatter

stupor – barely conscious, stunned

stealing over – taking over

vignette – a faint picture or illustration that blends in with its background

Sully – Thomas Sully, 19th-century portraitist

filigreed – delicate wire ornamental work

Moresque – Moorish or Arabic

countenance – face

fancy – imagination

confounded – amazed, perplexed, bewildered

eagerly the volume which discussed the paintings and their histories. Turning to the number which designated the oval portrait, I there read the vague and quaint words which follow:

"She was a maiden of rarest beauty, and not more lovely than full of glee. And evil was the hour when she saw, and loved, and wedded the painter. He, passionate, studious, **austere**, and having already a bride in his Art; she a maiden of rarest beauty, and not more lovely than full of glee; all light and smiles, and frolicsome as the young fawn; loving and cherishing all things; hating only the Art which was her rival; dreading only the **pallet** and brushes and other **untoward** instruments which deprived her of the countenance of her lover. It was thus a terrible thing for this lady to hear the painter speak of his desire to portray even his young bride. But she was humble and obedient, and sat meekly for many weeks in the dark, high turret-chamber where the light dripped upon the pale canvas only from overhead. But he, the painter, took glory in his work, which went on from hour to hour, and from day to day. And be was a passionate, and wild, and moody man, who became lost in **reveries**; so that he would not see that the light which fell so ghastly in that lone turret withered the health and the spirits of his bride, who **pined** visibly to all but him. Yet she smiled on and still on, uncomplainingly, because she saw that the painter (who had high renown) took a **fervid** and burning pleasure in his task, and wrought day and night to depict her who so loved him, yet who grew daily more dispirited and weak. And in **sooth** some who beheld the portrait spoke of its resemblance in low words, as of a mighty marvel, and a proof not less of the power of the painter than of his deep love for her whom he depicted so surpassingly well. But at length, as the labor drew nearer to its conclusion, there were admitted none into the turret; for the painter had grown wild with the **ardor** of his work, and turned his eyes from canvas merely, even to regard the countenance of his wife. And he would not see that the tints which he spread upon the canvas were drawn from the cheeks of her who sat beside him. And when many weeks bad passed, and but little remained to do, save one brush upon the mouth and one tint upon the eye, the spirit of the

agitation – anxiety, tension

austere – severe, bleak, stern

pallet – tablet that a painter holds and mixes pigments on

untoward – adverse, unfavorable, unseemly

reveries – daydreams

pined – suffered with longing, yearned deeply

fervid – passionate

sooth – truth

ardor – intensity of emotion

lady again flickered up as the flame within the socket of the lamp. And then the brush was given, and then the tint was placed; and, for one moment, the painter stood entranced before the work which he had wrought; but in the next, while he yet gazed, he grew **tremulous** and very **pallid**, and **aghast**, and crying with a loud voice, 'This is indeed Life itself!' turned suddenly to regard his beloved: She was dead!

tremulous – slightly shaking

pallid – pale, unhealthy looking

aghast – shocked, stupefied

The Oval Portrait

1. The story takes place in:
   A. England
   B. France
   C. Italy

2. The narrator is:
   A. wounded
   B. abandoned
   C. alone in the chateau

3. The narrator is fascinated by the portrait of a woman:
   A. in a studio
   B. in a book
   C. in his bedroom

4. The woman in the portrait is the artist's:
   A. wife
   B. fiancée
   C. mother

5. The woman apparently dies of:
   A. neglect
   B. inactivity
   C. shock

6. The word "*fancy*" (¶ 5) as used in the passage most nearly means:
   A. attraction
   B. decoration
   C. imagination

7. The narrative is best described as:
   A. a horror story
   B. a detective story
   C. a ghost story

8. The story thematically deals with:
   A. art versus life
   B. thwarted love
   C. marital discord

9. The woman can be best characterized as:
   A. uncomplaining
   B. entranced by art
   C. hostile

10. The portrait is described as:
    A. dream-like
    B. life-like
    C. idealized

Present at a Hanging
Ambrose Bierce 1888

An old man named Daniel Baker, living near Lebanon, Iowa, was suspected by his neighbors of having murdered a peddler who had obtained permission to pass the night at his house. This was in 1853, when peddling was more common in the Western country than it is now, and was attended with considerable danger. The peddler with his pack traversed the country by all manner of lonely roads, and was compelled to rely upon the country people for hospitality. This brought him into relation with queer characters, some of whom were not altogether **scrupulous** in their methods of making a living, murder being an acceptable means to that end. It occasionally occurred that a peddler with diminished pack and **swollen purse** would be traced to the lonely dwelling of some rough character and never could be traced beyond. This was so in the case of "old man Baker," as he was always called. (Such names are given in the western "settlements" only to elderly persons who are not esteemed; to the general disrepute of social unworth is affixed the special **reproach** of age.) A peddler came to his house and none went away--that is all that anybody knew.

Seven years later the Rev. Mr. Cummings, a Baptist minister well known in that part of the country, was driving by Baker's farm one night. It was not very dark: there was a bit of moon somewhere above the light veil of mist that lay along the earth. Mr. Cummings, who was at all times a cheerful person, was whistling a tune, which he would occasionally interrupt to speak a word of friendly encouragement to his horse. As he came to a little bridge across a dry ravine he saw the figure of a man standing upon it, clearly outlined against the gray background of a misty forest. The man had something strapped on his back and carried a heavy stick-- obviously an **itinerant** peddler. His attitude had in it a suggestion of abstraction, like that of a sleepwalker. Mr. Cummings reined in his horse when he arrived in front of him, gave him a pleasant **salutation** and invited him to a seat in the vehicle-- "if you are going my way," he added. The man raised his head, looked him full in the face, but neither answered nor

Ambrose Bierce – American editorialist, journalist, short story writer, fabulist, and satirist

scrupulous – moral, proper, principled

swollen purse – full wallet, monied

reproach – shame, rebuke

itinerant – traveling from place to place

salutation – greeting

made any further movement. The minister, with good-natured persistence, repeated his invitation. At this the man threw his right hand forward from his side and pointed downward as he stood on the extreme edge of the bridge. Mr. Cummings looked past him, over into the ravine, saw nothing unusual and withdrew his eyes to address the man again. He had disappeared. The horse, which all this time had been **uncommonly** restless, gave at the same moment a snort of terror and started to run away. Before he had regained control of the animal the minister was at the crest of the hill a hundred yards along. He looked back and saw the figure again, at the same place and in the same attitude as when he had first observed it. Then for the first time he was conscious of a sense of the supernatural and drove home as rapidly as his willing horse would go.

uncommonly – unusually

On arriving at home he related his adventure to his family, and early the next morning, accompanied by two neighbors, John White Corwell and Abner Raiser, returned to the spot. They found the body of old man Baker hanging by the neck from one of the beams of the bridge, immediately beneath the spot where the **apparition** had stood. A thick coating of dust, slightly dampened by the mist, covered the floor of the bridge, but the only footprints were those of Mr. Cummings' horse.

apparition – ghost, phantom

In taking down the body the men disturbed the loose, **friable** earth of the slope below it, disclosing human bones already nearly uncovered by the action of water and frost. They were identified as those of the lost peddler. At the double **inquest** the **coroner**'s jury found that Daniel Baker died by his own hand while suffering from temporary insanity, and that Samuel Morritz was murdered by some person or persons to the jury unknown.

friable – brittle, easily crumbled

inquest – official investigation into a person's cause of death

coroner – official authorized to determine the cause of suspicious or unusual deaths

Present at a Hanging

1. The townspeople of Lebanon think of Baker as a:
   - A. hermit
   - B. peddler
   - C. killer

2. The story is best described as a:
   - A. ghost story
   - B. folk tale
   - C. moralistic story

3. Daniel Baker was found to have died owing to:
   - A. insanity
   - B. suicide
   - C. drowning

4. The footprints found on the bridge belonged to:
   - A. the farmer, Daniel Baker
   - B. the minister, Mr. Cummings
   - C. a horse

5. The story covers a time period of:
   - A. one winter and spring
   - B. a year
   - C. seven years

6. The word *"itinerant"* (¶ 2) as used in the passage most nearly means:
   - A. beggar
   - B. lower class
   - C. wanderer

7. The name of the peddler is:
   - A. Abner Raiser
   - B. John White Corwell
   - C. Samuel Morritz

8. Daniel Baker died at the hands of:
   - A. a peddler
   - B. a mob
   - C. himself

9. The reverend's horse is:
   - A. restless
   - B. a nag
   - C. cooperative

10. The bones discovered are apparently those of:
    - A. Mr. Baker
    - B. the peddler
    - C. a stranger

Procuring Pleasant Dreams
Benjamin Franklin 1786

As a great part of our life is spent in sleep, during which we have sometimes pleasant and sometimes painful dreams, it becomes of some consequence to obtain the one kind and avoid the other; for whether real or imaginary, pain is pain and pleasure is pleasure. If we can sleep without dreaming, it is well that painful dreams are avoided. If, while we sleep, we can have any pleasant dreams, it is, as the French say, *autant de gagné*, so much added to the pleasure of life.

To this end it is, in the first place, necessary to be careful in preserving health by due exercise and great **temperance**; for in sickness the imagination is disturbed, and disagreeable, sometimes terrible, ideas are apt to present themselves. Exercise should precede meals, not immediately follow them; the first promotes, the latter, unless moderate, obstructs digestion. If, after exercise, we feed sparingly, the digestion will be easy and good, the body **lightsome**, the **temper** cheerful, and all the animal functions performed agreeably. Sleep, when it follows, will be natural and undisturbed, while **indolence**, with full feeding, occasions nightmares and horrors inexpressible; we fall from **precipices**, are assaulted by wild beasts, murderers, and demons, and experience every variety of distress. Observe, however, that the quantities of food and exercise are relative things: those who move much may, and indeed ought to, eat more; those who use little exercise should eat little. In general, mankind, since the improvement of cookery, eat about twice as much as nature requires. Suppers are not bad if we have not dined; but restless nights follow hearty suppers after full dinners. Indeed, as there is a difference in **constitutions**, some rest well after these meals; it costs them only a frightful dream and an **apoplexy**, after which they sleep till doomsday. Nothing is more common in the newspapers than instances of people who, after eating a hearty supper, are found dead abed in the morning.

Another means of preserving health to be attended to is the having a constant supply of fresh air in your bedchamber. It has been a great mistake, the sleeping in rooms exactly closed

Benjamin Franklin – called "the First American," one of the Founding Fathers of the United States

procuring – obtaining by particular care and effort

autant de gagné – all to the better (French)

temperance – sobriety, restraint in eating and drinking

lightsome – nimble

temper – state of mind, mood

indolence – laziness

precipices – steep rock faces

constitution – physical health and condition

apoplexy – great anger and excitement, stroke

and the beds surrounded by curtains. No outward air that may come in to you is so **unwholesome** as the unchanged air, often breathed, of a close chamber. As boiling water does not grow hotter by long boiling if the particles that receive greater heat can escape, so living bodies do not **putrefy** if the particles, so fast as they become putrid, can be thrown off. Nature expels them by the pores of the skin and lungs, and in a free, open air they are carried off; but in a close room we receive them again and again, though they become more and more corrupt. A number of persons crowded into a small room thus spoil the air in a few minutes, and even render it mortal as the **Black Hole at Calcutta**. A single person is said to spoil only a gallon of air per minute, and therefore requires a longer time to spoil a chamberful; but it is done, however, in proportion, and many **putrid** disorders hence have their origin. It is recorded of **Methuselah**, who, being the longest liver, may be supposed to have best preserved his health, that he slept always in the open air; for when he had lived five hundred years an angel said to him: "Arise, Methuselah, and build thee an house, for thou shalt live yet five hundred years longer." But Methuselah answered and said: "If I am to live but five hundred years longer, it is not worthwhile to build me an house; I will sleep in the air, as I have been used to do." Physicians, after having for ages contended that the sick should not be **indulged** with fresh air, have at length discovered that it may do them good. It is therefore to be hoped that they may in time discover likewise that it is not hurtful to those who are in health, and that we may then be cured of the *aerophobia* that at present distresses weak minds, and makes them choose to be stifled and poisoned rather than leave open the window of a bedchamber or put down the **glass of a coach**.

Confined air, when saturated with **perspirable** matter, will not receive more, and that matter must remain in our bodies and occasion diseases; but it gives us some previous notice of its being about to be hurtful by producing certain uneasiness, slight indeed at first, such as with regard to the lungs is a **trifling** sensation and to the pores of the skin a kind of restlessness which is difficult to describe, and few that feel it know the cause of it. But we may recollect that sometimes, on

unwholesome – unhealthy

putrefy – rot, decay

Black Hole of Calcutta – 14'-by-18' room in a colonial Indian fort where 146 British POWs were reportedly crammed, of whom 23 men survived the night of June 20, 1756

putrid – rotten, foul smelling

Methuselah – the oldest man in the Bible, said to have lived to age 969

indulged – allowed as a special pleasure, even if unhealthy

aerophobia – abnormal fear of drafts or fresh air

glass of a coach – window of a carriage

perspirable – sweaty, emitting perspiration

trifling – insignificant, unimportant

waking in the night, we have, if warmly covered, found it difficult to get asleep again. We turn often, without finding repose in any position. This fidgetiness (to use a vulgar expression for want of a better) is **occasioned** wholly by uneasiness in the skin, owing to the retention of the perspirable matter, the **bedclothes** having received their quantity, and being saturated, refusing to take any more. To become **sensible** of this by an experiment, let a person keep his position in the bed, throw off the bedclothes, and **suffer** fresh air to approach the part uncovered of his body; he will then feel that part suddenly refreshed, for the air will immediately relieve the skin by receiving, licking up, and carrying off the load of perspirable matter that approaches the warm skin, in receiving its part of that vapor, receives therewith a degree of heat that **rarefies** and renders it lighter, by cooler and therefore heavier fresh air, which for a moment supplies its place, and then, being likewise changed and warmed, gives way to a succeeding quantity.

occasioned – caused

bedclothes – sleepwear

sensible – cognizant, aware

suffer – allow, permit

rarefies – makes less dense

This is the order of nature to prevent animals being infected by their own perspiration. He will now be sensible of the difference between the part exposed to the air and that which, remaining sunk in the bed, denies the air access; for this part now **manifests** its uneasiness more distinctly by the comparison, and the **seat** of the uneasiness is more plainly perceived than when the whole surface of the body was affected by it.

manifests – shows, displays

seat – location

Here, then, is one great and general cause of unpleasing dreams. For when the body is uneasy the mind will be disturbed by it, and disagreeable ideas of various kinds will in sleep be the natural consequences. The remedies, preventive and curative, follow.

1. By eating moderately (as before advised for health's sake) less perspirable matter is produced in a given time; hence the bedclothes receive it longer before they are saturated, and we may therefore sleep longer before we are made uneasy by their refusing to receive any more.

2. By using thinner and more porous bedclothes, which will suffer the perspirable matter more easily to pass through them, we are less incommoded, such being longer tolerable.

3. When you are awakened by this uneasiness and find you cannot easily sleep again, get out of bed, beat up and turn your pillow, shake the bedclothes well, with at least twenty shakes, then throw the bed open and leave it to cool; in the meanwhile, continuing undressed, walk about your chamber till your skin has had time to discharge its load, which it will do sooner as the air may be dryer and colder. When you begin to feel the cold air unpleasant, then return to your bed and you will soon fall asleep, and your sleep will be sweet and pleasant. All the scenes presented to your **fancy** will be, too, of a pleasing kind. I am often as agreeably entertained with them as by the scenery of an opera. If you happen to be too **indolent** to get out of bed, you may, instead of it, lift up your bedclothes with one arm and leg, so as to draw in a good deal of fresh air, and by letting them fall force it out again. This, repeated twenty times, will so clear them of the perspirable matter they have **imbibed** as to permit your sleeping well for some time afterward. But this latter method is not equal to the former.

fancy – imagination

indolent – lazy, lethargic

imbibed – drunk, consumed

Those who do not love trouble and can afford to have two beds will find great luxury in rising, when they wake in a hot bed, and going into the cool one. Such shifting of beds would also be of great service to persons ill of a fever, as it refreshes and frequently procures sleep. A very large bed that will admit a removal so distant from the first situation as to be cool and sweet may in a degree answer the same end.

One or two observations more will conclude this little piece. Care must be taken, when you lie down, to **dispose** your pillow so as to suit your manner of placing your head and to be perfectly easy; then place your limbs so as not to bear inconveniently hard upon one another, as, for instance, the joints of your ankles; for though a bad position may at first give but little pain and be hardly noticed, yet a continuance will render it less tolerable, and the uneasiness may come on while you are asleep and disturb your imagination. These are

dispose – arrange

the rules of the art. But though they will generally prove effectual in producing the end intended, there is a case in which the most **punctual** observance of them will be totally fruitless. I need not mention the case to you, my dear friend; but my account of the art would be imperfect without it. The case is when the person who desires to have pleasant dreams has not taken care to preserve, what is necessary above all things,

A GOOD CONSCIENCE.

punctual – precise, prompt

Procuring Pleasant Dreams

1. Franklin says the important key for pleasant dreams is good:
   A. health
   B. digestion
   C. habits of thought

2. Franklin claims the main cause of nightmares is too much:
   A. inactivity
   B. drinking
   C. dinner

3. The most desirable thing for comfortable sleep is said to be:
   A. a bed companion
   B. clean bedclothes
   C. fresh air

4. Tossing-and-turning stems from bedclothes that are:
   A. loose-fitting
   B. sweaty
   C. tight-fitting

5. Good sleep is said to be promoted above all by:
   A. a darkened room
   B. a clear conscience
   C. quiet nerves

6. The word "*suffer*" (¶ 4) as used in the passage most nearly means:
   A. admit
   B. agonize
   C. stifle

7. Two beds or one large bed are recommended for:
   A. married couples
   B. over-heating
   C. nightmares

8. Mankind eats double what is needed owing to:
   A. lack of exercise
   B. improved cooking
   C. poor sleep thereafter

9. Long-lived Methuselah reportedly insisted on:
   A. light meals
   B. sleeping outdoors
   C. avoiding heavy suppers

10. The major source of unpleasant dreams is said to be:
   A. a guilty conscience
   B. disturbing thoughts
   C. an uncomfortable pillow

The Bible: The Prodigal Son
Luke 15:11-32 circa 80-85

1 Now the tax collectors and sinners were all drawing near to hear him.
2 And the **Pharisees** and the scribes murmured, saying, "This man receives sinners and eats with them."
3 So he told them this **parable**:

*****

11 And he said, "There was a man who had two sons;
12 and the younger of them said to his father, "Father, give me the share of property that falls to me.' And he divided his living between them.
13 Not many days later, the younger son gathered all he had and took his journey into a far country, and there he **squandered** his property in loose living.
14 And when he had spent everything, a great **famine** arose in that country, and he began to be in want.
15 So he went and joined himself to one of the citizens of that country, who sent him into his fields to feed swine.
16 And he would gladly have fed on the pods that the swine ate; and no one gave him anything.
17 But when he came to himself he said, "How many of my father's hired servants have bread enough and to spare, but I perish here with hunger!
18 I will arise and go to my father, and I will say to him, "Father, I have sinned against heaven and before you;
19 I am no longer worthy to be called your son; treat me as one of your hired servants.'"
20 And he arose and came to his father. But while he was yet at a distance, his father saw him and had compassion, and ran and embraced him and kissed him.
21 And the son said to him, "Father, I have sinned against heaven and before you; I am no longer worthy to be called your son.'
22 But the father said to his servants, "Bring quickly the best robe, and put it on him; and put a ring on his hand, and shoes on his feet;
23 and bring the fatted calf and kill it, and let us eat and make

prodigal – spendthrift, wastefully or recklessly extravagant

Pharisees – Jewish sect, the strict ruling class of Israel, with whom Jesus was in constant conflict

parable – a simple story used to teach a moral or spiritual lesson

squander – waste money in a reckless or foolish manner

famine – extreme scarcity of food in a region

143

merry;

24 for this my son was dead, and is alive again; he was lost, and is found.' And they began to make merry.

25 "Now his elder son was in the field; and as he came and drew near to the house, he heard music and dancing.

26 And he called one of the servants and asked what this meant.

27 And he said to him, "Your brother has come, and your father has killed the fatted calf, because he has received him safe and sound.'

28 But he was angry and refused to go in. His father came out and **entreated** him,

29 but he answered his father, "Lo, these many years I have served you, and I never disobeyed your command; yet you never gave me a **kid**, that I might make merry with my friends.

30 But when this son of yours came, who has devoured your living with **harlots**, you killed for him the fatted calf!'

31 And he said to him, "Son, you are always with me, and all that is mine is yours.

32 It was fitting to make merry and be glad, for this your brother was dead, and is alive; he was lost, and is found.'"

entreat – ask earnestly or anxiously, plead, implore

kid – young goat

harlot – prostitute, woman who sleeps around

The Bible: The Prodigal Son

1. The word "*prodigal*" describes someone who is:
   A. returning
   B. disrespectful
   C. wasteful

2. The prodigal son's departure is financed by:
   A. a theft
   B. an inheritance
   C. a gift

3. In a far country the younger son ends up:
   A. toiling as a slave
   B. feeding livestock
   C. feeling homesick

4. The older brother reacts to his sibling's reception with:
   A. thankfulness
   B. resentment
   C. brotherly love

5. His father treats the returning son generously because the boy realizes his:
   A. sinfulness
   B. ingratitude
   C. carelessness

6. The word "*entreat*" (l. 28) as used in the passage most nearly means:
   A. reward
   B. plead
   C. invite

7. The son asks his father to treat him like:
   A. a sinner
   B. a paid servant
   C. his older brother

8. This passage may best be categorized as a:
   A. religious fable
   B. parable
   C. psalm

9. The prodigal son, before returning home, confronts:
   A. divine disfavor
   B. bad omens
   C. hunger

10. The father first gives his prodigal son:
   A. clothing
   B. a fatted calf
   C. a kiss

Scott's Last Diary Entries
Robert F. Scott 1912

Accompanied by 16 men, Robert Falcon Scott led a doomed British expedition in a race to the South Pole. They arrived only to discover they had been preceded to the pole by 34 days by Norwegian Roald Amundsen.

March 29th, 1912

The causes of the disaster are not due to faulty organisation, but to misfortune in all risks which had to be undertaken.

1. The loss of pony transport in March 1911 **obliged** me to start later than I had intended, and obliged the limits of stuff transported to be narrowed.

obliged – forced, required, necessitated constrained

2. The weather throughout the outward journey, and especially the long gale in 83° S., stopped us.

3. The soft snow in lower reaches of glacier again reduced pace.

We fought these **untoward** events with a will and conquered, but it cut into our **provision reserve**.

untoward – unfavorable or unfortunate

provision reserve – food and/or supplies saved for future use

Every detail of our food supplies, clothing and **depots** made on the interior ice-sheet and over that long stretch of 700 miles to the Pole and back, worked out to perfection. The advance party would have returned to the glacier in fine form and with surplus of food, but for the astonishing failure of the man whom we had least expected to fail. Edgar Evans was thought the strongest man of the party.

depot – place for storage of supplies and equipment, depository

The Beardmore Glacier is not difficult in fine weather, but on our return we did not get a single completely fine day; this with a sick companion enormously increased our anxieties. As I have said elsewhere we got into frightfully rough ice and Edgar Evans received a concussion of the brain – he died a natural death, but left us a shaken party with the season unduly advanced.

But all the facts above enumerated were as nothing to the surprise which awaited us on the **Barrier**. I maintain that our arrangements for returning were quite adequate, and that no one in the world would have expected the temperatures and surfaces which we encountered at this time of the year. On the summit in lat. 85° 86° we had -20°, -30°. On the Barrier in lat. 82°, 10,000 feet lower, we had -30° in the day, -47° at night pretty regularly, with continuous head wind during our day marches. It is clear that these circumstances come on very suddenly, and our wreck is certainly due to this sudden advent of severe weather, which does not seem to have any satisfactory cause. I do not think human beings ever came through such a month as we have come through, and we should have got through in spite of the weather but for the sickening of a second companion, Captain Oates, and a shortage of fuel in our depots for which I cannot account, and finally, but for the storm which has fallen on us within 11 miles of the depot at which we hoped to secure our final supplies. Surely misfortune could scarcely have exceeded this last blow. We arrived within 11 miles of our old One Ton Camp with fuel for one last meal and food for two days. For four days we have been unable to leave the tent – the **gale** howling about us. We are weak, writing is difficult, but for my own sake I do not regret this journey, which has shown that Englishmen can endure hardships, help one another, and meet death with as great a **fortitude** as ever in the past. We took risks, we knew we took them; things have come out against us, and therefore we have no cause for complaint, but bow to the will of **Providence,** determined still to do our best to the last. But if we have been willing to give our lives to this enterprise, which is for the honour of our country, I appeal to our countrymen to see that those who depend on us are properly cared for.

Had we lived, I should have had a tale to tell of the hardihood, endurance, and courage of my companions which would have stirred the heart of every Englishman. These rough notes and our dead bodies must tell the tale, but surely, surely, a great rich country like ours will see that those who are dependent on us are properly provided for.

Barrier – today called the Ross Ice Shelf

gale – very strong wind

fortitude – courage in pain or adversity

Providence – the protective care of God

147

March 29th, 1912

Since the 21st we have had a continuous gale from W.S.W. and S.W. We had fuel to make two cups of tea apiece and bare food for two days on the 20th. Every day we have been ready to start for our depot 11 miles away, but outside the door of the tent it remains a scene of whirling drift. I do not think we can hope for any better things now. We shall stick it out to the end, but we are getting weaker, of course, and the end cannot be far.

It seems a pity, but I do not think I can write more.

R. SCOTT.

For God's sake look after our people.

Scott's Last Diary Entries

1. Scott's expedition initially relied on these for his team's polar transportation:
   - A. huskies
   - B. ponies
   - C. Inuit natives' sleds

2. Scott's nationality is:
   - A. American
   - B. Norwegian
   - C. English

3. The expedition's goal was:
   - A. to be first to the North Pole
   - B. to be first to the South Pole
   - C. to claim and map the pole

4. The first one to perish, Edgar Evans, is said to have died:
   - A. from a fall
   - B. of pneumonia
   - C. natural causes

5. Scott attributes the expedition's failure primarily to poor:
   - A. planning
   - B. weather
   - C. navigation aids

6. As the end nears, Scott is lastly concerned about the men's:
   - A. honor
   - B. reputation
   - C. families

7. The word "*untoward*" (¶ 2) in context most nearly means:
   - A. dishonest
   - B. winding
   - C. unfavorable

8. The word "*Providence*" (¶ 4) refers to:
   - A. fate
   - B. God
   - C. luck

9. Scott's final wish (last line) is that "our people" be looked after, indicating namely the:
   - A. expedition survivors
   - B. expedition backers
   - C. crew's relatives

10. The problem encountered with the Beardmore Glacier is:
   - A. intolerably frigid conditions
   - B. steepness
   - C. soft snow

The Secret Life of Walter Mitty
James Thurber 1939

"We're going through!" The Commander's voice was like thin ice breaking. He wore his full-dress uniform, with the heavily braided white cap pulled down **rakishly** over one cold gray eye. "We can't make it, sir. It's spoiling for a hurricane, if you ask me." "I'm not asking you, Lieutenant Berg," said the Commander. "Throw on the power lights! Rev her up to 8,500! We're going through!" The pounding of the cylinders increased: ta-pocketa-pocketa-pocketa-pocketa-pocketa. The Commander stared at the ice forming on the pilot window. He walked over and twisted a row of complicated dials. "Switch on No. 8 **auxiliary**!" he shouted. "Switch on No. 8 auxiliary!" repeated Lieutenant Berg. "Full strength in No. 3 turret!" shouted the Commander. "Full strength in No. 3 turret!" The crew, bending to their various tasks in the huge, hurtling eight-engined Navy **hydroplane**, looked at each other and grinned. "The Old Man'll get us through," they said to one another. "The Old Man ain't afraid of Hell!" ...

"Not so fast! You're driving too fast!" said Mrs. Mitty. "What are you driving so fast for?"

"Hmm?" said Walter Mitty. He looked at his wife, in the seat beside him, with shocked astonishment. She seemed grossly unfamiliar, like a strange woman who had yelled at him in a crowd. "You were up to fifty-five," she said. "You know I don't like to go more than forty. You were up to fifty-five." Walter Mitty drove on toward Waterbury in silence, the roaring of the SN202 through the worst storm in twenty years of Navy flying fading in the remote, intimate airways of his mind. "You're tensed up again," said Mrs. Mitty. "It's one of your days. I wish you'd let Dr. Renshaw look you over."

Walter Mitty stopped the car in front of the building where his wife went to have her hair done. "Remember to get those **overshoes** while I'm having my hair done," she said. "I don't need overshoes," said Mitty. She put her mirror back into her bag. "We've been all through that," she said, getting out of

James Thurber – cartoonist, wit, playwright, known for short stories and cartoons published in *The New Yorker* magazine

rakish – dashing, debonair, jaunty

auxiliary – back up, reserve in case of need

hydroplane – a boat designed to move over the surface of water at very high speeds, seaplane

overshoes – galoshes, rubber covering placed over shoes for rain or snow protection

the car. "You're not a young man any longer." He raced the engine a little. "Why don't you wear your gloves? Have you lost your gloves?" Walter Mitty reached in a pocket and brought out the gloves. He put them on, but after she had turned and gone into the building and he had driven on to a red light, he took them off again. "Pick it up, brother!" snapped a cop as the light changed, and Mitty hastily pulled on his gloves and lurched ahead. He drove around the streets aimlessly for a time, and then he drove past the hospital on his way to the parking lot.

... "It's the millionaire banker, Wellington McMillan," said the pretty nurse. "Yes?" said Walter Mitty, removing his gloves slowly. "Who has the case?" "Dr. Renshaw and Dr. Benbow, but there are two specialists here, Dr. Remington from New York and Dr. Pritchard-Mitford from London. He flew over." A door opened down a long, cool corridor and Dr. Renshaw came out. He looked **distraught** and **haggard**. "Hello, Mitty," he said. "We're having the devil's own time with McMillan, the millionaire banker and close personal friend of Roosevelt. **Obstreosis** of the ductal tract. **Tertiary.** Wish you'd take a look at him." "Glad to," said Mitty.

In the operating room there were whispered introductions: "Dr. Remington, Dr. Mitty. Dr. Pritchard-Mitford, Dr. Mitty." "I've read your book on **streptothricosis**," said Pritchard-Mitford, shaking hands. "A brilliant performance, sir." "Thank you," said Walter Mitty. "Didn't know you were in the States, Mitty," grumbled Remington. "**Coals to Newcastle**, bringing Mitford and me up here for a tertiary." "You are very kind," said Mitty. A huge, complicated machine, connected to the operating table, with many tubes and wires, began at this moment to go pocketa-pocketa-pocketa. "The new anaesthetizer is giving way!" shouted an interne. "There is no one in the East who knows how to fix it!" "Quiet, man!" said Mitty, in a low, cool voice. He sprang to the machine, which was now going pocketa-pocketa-queep-pocketa-queep. He began fingering delicately a row of glistening dials. "Give me a fountain pen!" he snapped. Someone handed him a fountain pen. He pulled a faulty piston out of the machine and inserted the pen in its place.

distraught – deeply troubled or anguished

haggard – with a gaunt or very tired appearance

obstreosis – imagined blockage disease – (actually a species of flower)

tertiary – needing specialized care

streptothricosis – imaginary infection

Coals to Newcastle – a pointless enterprise, since Newcastle was already a coal-rich mining town

151

"That will hold for ten minutes," he said. "Get on with the operation." A nurse hurried over and whispered to Renshaw, and Mitty saw the man turn pale. "**Coreopsis** has set in," said Renshaw nervously. "If you would take over, Mitty?" Mitty looked at him and at the **craven** figure of Benbow, who drank, and at the grave, uncertain faces of the two great specialists. "If you wish," he said. They slipped a white gown on him; he adjusted a mask and drew on thin gloves; nurses handed him shining ..."Back it up, Mac! Look out for that Buick!" Walter Mitty jammed on the brakes. "Wrong lane, Mac," said the parking-lot attendant, looking at Mitty closely. "Gee. Yeh," muttered Mitty. He began cautiously to back out of the lane marked "Exit Only." "Leave her sit there," said the attendant. "I'll put her away." Mitty got out of the car. "Hey, better leave the key." "Oh," said Mitty, handing the man the ignition key. The attendant vaulted into the car, backed it up with **insolent** skill, and put it where it belonged.

They're so damn **cocky**, thought Walter Mitty, walking along Main Street; they think they know everything. Once he had tried to take his chains off, outside **New Milford,** and he had got them wound around the axles. A man had had to come out in a wrecking car and unwind them, a young, grinning garageman. Since then Mrs. Mitty always made him drive to a garage to have the chains taken off. The next time, he thought, I'll wear my right arm in a sling; they won't grin at me then. I'll have my right arm in a sling and they'll see I couldn't possibly take the chains off myself. He kicked at the slush on the sidewalk. "Overshoes," he said to himself, and he began looking for a shoe store.

When he came out into the street again, with the overshoes in a box under his arm, Walter Mitty began to wonder what the other thing was his wife had told him to get. She had told him, twice, before they set out from their house for **Waterbury**. In a way he hated these weekly trips to town—he was always getting something wrong. Kleenex, he thought, **Squibb's**, razor blades? No. Toothpaste, toothbrush, bicarbonate, **carborundum**, **initiative** and **referendum**? He gave it up. But she would remember it. "Where's the what's-its-name?" she would ask. "Don't tell me you forgot the

coreopsis – imaginary disease (actually a daisy-like kind of flower)

craven – cowardly, timid

insolent – disrespectful, rude, arrogant

cocky – arrogant, brashly self-confident

New Milford – suburban town in Connecticut

Waterbury – town in Connecticut

Squibb's – mineral oil pharmacy product

*****carborundum**– carbon-based abrasive

*****initiative** – procedure for citizens to propose and vote on a law

*****referendum** – ballot question for voters

*** (Mitty's confusion of similar sounding errands)

152

what's-its-name." A newsboy went by shouting something about the Waterbury trial.

... "Perhaps this will refresh your memory." The District Attorney suddenly thrust a heavy automatic at the quiet figure on the witness stand. "Have you ever seen this before?" Walter Mitty took the gun and examined it expertly. "This is my Webley-Vickers 50.80," he said calmly. An excited buzz ran around the courtroom. The Judge rapped for order. "You are a crack shot with any sort of firearms, I believe?" said the District Attorney, insinuatingly. "Objection!" shouted Mitty's attorney. "We have shown that the defendant could not have fired the shot. We have shown that he wore his right arm in a sling on the night of the fourteenth of July." Walter Mitty raised his hand briefly and the bickering attorneys were stilled. "With any known make of gun," he said evenly, "I could have killed Gregory Fitzhurst at three hundred feet *with my left hand*." **Pandemonium** broke loose in the courtroom. A woman's scream rose above the **bedlam** and suddenly a lovely, dark-haired girl was in Walter Mitty's arms. The District Attorney struck at her savagely. Without rising from his chair, Mitty let the man have it on the point of the chin. "You miserable **cur!**"...

> **pandemonium** – chaos, great disorder
>
> **bedlam** – uproar, turmoil, madhouse
>
> **cur** – mongrel (non-pure-breed) dog

"Puppy biscuit," said Walter Mitty. He stopped walking and the buildings of Waterbury rose up out of the misty courtroom and surrounded him again. A woman who was passing laughed. "He said 'Puppy biscuit,'" she said to her companion. "That man said 'Puppy biscuit' to himself."

Walter Mitty hurried on. He went into an A. & P., not the first one he came to but a smaller one farther up the street. "I want some biscuit for small, young dogs," he said to the clerk. "Any special brand, sir?" The greatest pistol shot in the world thought a moment. "It says 'Puppies Bark for It' on the box," said Walter Mitty.

His wife would be through at the hairdresser's in fifteen minutes, Mitty saw in looking at his watch, unless they had trouble drying it; sometimes they had trouble drying it. She didn't like to get to the hotel first; she would want him to be there waiting for her as usual. He found a big leather chair in the lobby, facing a window, and he put the overshoes and the puppy biscuit on the floor beside it. He picked up an old copy of *Liberty* and sank down into the chair. "Can Germany Conquer the World Through the Air?" Walter Mitty looked at the pictures of bombing planes and of ruined streets.

. . ."The cannonading has got the wind up in young Raleigh, sir," said the sergeant. Captain Mitty looked up at him through **touselled** hair. "Get him to bed," he said wearily. "With the others. I'll fly alone." "But you can't, sir," said the sergeant anxiously. "It takes two men to handle that bomber and the Archies are pounding hell out of the air. Von Richtman's **circus** is between here and Saulier." "Somebody's got to get that ammunition dump," said Mitty. "I'm going over. Spot of brandy?" He poured a drink for the sergeant and one for himself. War thundered and whined around the dugout and battered at the door. There was a rending of wood and splinters flew through the room. "A bit of a near thing," said Captain Mitty carelessly. "The box **barrage** is closing in," said the sergeant. "We only live once, Sergeant," said Mitty, with his faint, fleeting smile. "Or do we?" He poured another brandy and tossed it off. "I never see a man could hold his brandy like you, sir," said the sergeant. "Begging your pardon, sir." Captain Mitty stood up and strapped on his huge Webley-Vickers automatic. "It's forty kilometres through hell, sir," said the sergeant. Mitty finished one last brandy. "After all," he said softly, "what isn't?" The pounding of the cannon increased; there was the rat-tat-tatting of machine guns, and from somewhere came the menacing pocketa-pocketa-pocketa of the new flame-throwers. Walter Mitty walked to the door of the dugout humming "**Auprès de Ma Blonde**." He turned and waved to the sergeant. "Cheerio!" he said. ...

Something struck his shoulder. "I've been looking all over this hotel for you," said Mrs. Mitty. "Why do you have to hide in this old chair? How did you expect me to find you?" "Things close in," said Walter Mitty vaguely. "What?" Mrs. Mitty said. "Did you get the what's-its-name? The puppy

touselled – untidy, disheveled, messy

circus – airplane squadron

barrage – heavy artillery fire

"**Auprès de Ma Blonde**" ("**Next to My Girlfriend**") – military parade song

biscuit? What's in that box?" "Overshoes," said Mitty. "Couldn't you have put them on in the store?" "I was thinking," said Walter Mitty. "Does it ever occur to you that I am sometimes thinking?" She looked at him. "I'm going to take your temperature when I get you home," she said.'

They went out through the revolving doors that made a faintly **derisive** whistling sound when you pushed them. It was two blocks to the parking lot. At the drugstore on the corner she said, "Wait here for me. I forgot something. I won't be a minute." She was more than a minute. Walter Mitty lighted a cigarette. It began to rain, rain with sleet in it. He stood up against the wall of the drugstore, smoking. ... He put his shoulders back and his heels together. "To hell with the handkerchief," said Walter Mitty scornfully. He took one last drag on his cigarette and snapped it away. Then, with that faint, fleeting smile playing about his lips, he faced the firing squad; erect and motionless, proud and disdainful, Walter Mitty the Undefeated, **inscrutable** to the last.

derisive – ridiculing or scorning

inscrutable – not readily interpreted or understood, mystifying

The Secret Life of Walter Mitty

1. Mitty's wife is portrayed as:
   A. scatter-brained
   B. nagging
   C. henpecked

2. Mitty fixes the anesthetizer with a:
   A. pen
   B. rubber band
   C. tongue depressor

3. Mitty contemplates wearing a sling on his right arm to:
   A. attract attention
   B. get sympathy
   C. avoid ridicule

4. In addition to overshoes, Mitty purchases:
   A. Kleenex
   B. dog biscuits
   C. *Liberty* magazine

5. The story closes with Mitty imagining himself being:
   A. single
   B. star of a movie
   C. executed

6. The word *"craven"* (¶ 5) used in the passage most nearly means:
   A. desired
   B. cowardly
   C. wicked

7. In the opening paragraph, Commander Mitty is piloting:
   A. a military aircraft
   B. a speedboat
   C. a submarine

8. Webley-Vickers 50.80 is a:
   A. bomber
   B. pistol
   C. race car

9. The general tone of the story is:
   A. humorous
   B. sarcastic
   C. mocking

10. Mitty's everyday life would seem to be:
    A. adventurous
    B. dull
    C. momentous

A Slander
Anton Chekhov circa 1922

Anton Chekhov – Russian physician, dramaturge and author, considered one of the greatest short story writers

Serge Kapitonich Ahineev, the writing master, was marrying his daughter to the teacher of history and geography. The wedding festivities were going off most successfully. In the drawing room there was singing, playing, and dancing. Waiters hired from the club were flitting distractedly about the rooms, dressed in black **swallowtails** and dirty white ties. There was a continual hubub and **din** of conversation. Sitting side by side on the sofa, the teacher of mathematics, the French teacher, and the junior assessor of taxes were talking hurriedly and interrupting one another as they described to the guests cases of persons being buried alive, and gave their opinions on spiritualism. None of them believed in spiritualism, but all admitted that there were many things in this world which would always be beyond the mind of man. In the next room the literature master was explaining to the visitors the cases in which a sentry has the right to fire on passers-by. The subjects, as you perceive, were alarming, but very agreeable. Persons whose social position **precluded** them from entering were looking in at the windows from the yard. Just at midnight the master of the house went into the kitchen to see whether everything was ready for supper. The kitchen from floor to ceiling was filled with fumes composed of goose, duck, and many other odors. On two tables the accessories, the drinks and light refreshments, were set out in artistic disorder. The cook, Marfa, a red-faced woman whose figure was like a barrel with a belt around it, was bustling about the tables of the assistant usher, Vankin. "Who is it? A-a-h! . . . Delighted to meet you! Sergei Kapitonich! You're a fine grandfather, I must say!"

"I'm not kissing," said Ahineev in confusion. "Who told you so, you fool? I was only . . . I smacked my lips . . . in reference to . . . as an indication of. . . pleasure . . . at the sight of the fish."

"**Tell that to the marines!**" The intrusive face vanished, wearing a broad grin.

slander – an untruthful statement about a person that harms the person's reputation or standing in the community

swallowtail – a formal white-tie tailcoat

din – a loud, unpleasant, and prolonged noise

preclude – prevent from happening, make impossible

tell that to the marines! – a scornful response to an incredible story

Ahineev flushed.

"Hang it!" he thought, "the beast will go now and talk scandal. He'll disgrace me to all the town, the brute."

Ahineev went timidly into the drawing room and looked stealthily round for Vankin. Vankin was standing by the piano, and, bending down with a **jaunty** air, was whispering something to the inspector's sister-in-law, who was laughing.

"Talking about me!" thought Ahineev. "About me, blast him! And she believes it . . . believes it! She laughs! Mercy on us! No, I can't let it pass . . . I can't. I must do something to prevent his being believed. . . . I'll speak to them all, and he'll be shown up for a fool and a gossip."

Ahineev scratched his head, and still overcome with embarrassment, went up to the French teacher.

"I've just been in the kitchen to see after the supper," he said to the Frenchman. "I know you are fond of fish, and I've a **sturgeon**, my dear fellow, beyond everything! A yard and a half long! Ha, ha, ha! And, by the way . . . I was just forgetting. . . . In the kitchen just now, with that sturgeon . . . quite a little story! I went into the kitchen just now and wanted to look at the supper dishes. I looked at the sturgeon and I smacked my lips with relish . . . at the **piquancy** of it. And at the very moment that fool Vankin came in and said: . . . 'Ha, ha, ha! . . . So you're kissing here!' Kissing Marfa, the cook! What a thing to imagine, silly fool! The woman is a perfect fright, like all the beasts put together, and he talks about kissing! Queer fish!"

"Who's a queer fish?" asked the mathematics teacher, coming up.

"Why he, over there – Vankin! I went into the kitchen . . ."

And he told the story of Vankin. ". . . He amused me, queer fish! I'd rather kiss a dog than Marfa, if you ask me," added

Ahineev. He looked round and saw behind him the junior assessor of taxes.

"We were talking of Vankin," he said. "Queer fish, he is! He went into the kitchen, saw me beside Marfa, and began inventing all sorts of silly stories. 'Why are you kissing?' he says. He must have had a drop too much. 'And I'd rather kiss a turkeycock than Marfa,' I said, 'And I've a wife of my own, you fool,' said I. He did amuse me!"

"Who amused you?" asked the priest who taught Scripture in the school, going up to Ahineev.

"Vankin. I was standing in the kitchen, you know, looking at the sturgeon. . . ."

And so on. Within half an hour or so all the guests knew the incident of the sturgeon and Vankin.

"Let him tell away now!" thought Ahineev, rubbing his hands. "Let him! He'll begin telling his story and they'll say to him at once, 'Enough of your improbable nonsense, you fool, we know all about it!"

And Ahineev was so relieved that in his joy he drank four glasses too many. After escorting the young people to their room, he went to bed and slept like an innocent babe, and next day he thought no more of the incident with the sturgeon. But, alas! man proposes, but God disposes. An evil tongue did its evil work, and Ahineev's strategy was of no avail. Just a week later--to be precise, on Wednesday after the third lesson--when Ahineev was standing in the middle of the teacher's room, holding forth on the vicious propensities of a boy called Visekin, the headmaster went up to him and drew him aside:

"Look here, Sergei Kapitonich," said the headmaster, "you must excuse me. . . . It's not my business; but all the same I must make you realize. . . . It's my duty. You see, there are rumors that you are romancing with that . . . cook. . . . It's nothing to do with me, but . . . flirt with her, kiss her . . . as you please, but don't let it be so public, please. I entreat you! Don't forget that you're a schoolmaster."

Ahineev turned cold and faint. He went home like a man stung by a whole swarm of bees, like a man scalded with boiling water. As he walked home, it seemed to him that the whole town was looking at him as though he were smeared with **pitch**. At home fresh trouble awaited him.

"Why aren't you gobbling up your food as usual?" his wife asked him at dinner. "What are you so **pensive** about? Brooding over your **amours**? Pining for your Marfa? I know all about it, Mohammedan! Kind friends have opened my eyes! O-o-o! . . . you savage !"

And she slapped him in the face. He got up from the table, not feeling the earth under his feet, and without his hat or coat, made his way to Vankin. He found him at home.

"You **scoundrel**!" he addressed him. "Why have you covered me with mud before all the town? Why did you set this slander going about me?"

"What slander? What are you talking about?"

"Who was it gossiped of my kissing Marfa? Wasn't it you? Tell me that. Wasn't it you, you **brigand**?"

Vankin blinked and twitched in every fiber of his battered **countenance**, raised his eyes to the icon and articulated, "God blast me! Strike me blind and lay me out, if I said a single word about you! May I be left without house and home, may I be stricken with worse than **cholera**!"

Vankin's sincerity did not admit of doubt. It was evidently not he who was the author of the slander.

"But who, then, who?" Ahineev wondered, going over all his acquaintances in his mind and beating himself on the breast. "Who, then?"

pitch – thick, dark, sticky substance obtained from the distillation residue of tar

pensive – lost in thought, reflective

amours – secret or illicit love affairs or lovers

scoundrel – an unprincipled, dishonorable person; villain

brigand – a bandit or plunderer

countenance – face or facial expression

cholera – an infectious disease that can cause severe diarrhea, dehydration, and death

A Slander

1. The "slander" against Ahineev is that he is:
   A. a "queer" fish
   B. a gossip
   C. the cook's lover

2. Ahineev's role at the party is to:
   A. host a wedding
   B. receive an award
   C. oversee the kitchen

3. Ahineev is, first off, berated for his behavior by:
   A. Vankin
   B. his wife
   C. the headmaster

4. Ahineev drinks "four glasses too many" out of a feeling of:
   A. joy
   B. embarrassment
   C. jitteriness

5. The originator of the slanderous story is apparently:
   A. Vankin
   B. Marfa
   C. Ahineev

6. The word "*pensive*" (16 lines from the end) as used in the passage most nearly means:
   A. contemplative
   B. irritated
   C. paranoid

7. The subjects discussed by the guests are said to be:
   A. alarming
   B. disagreeable
   C. ordinary

8. Ahineev visits Vankin to discover if Vankin is:
   A. a slanderer
   B. involved with Marfa
   C. seeking Ahineev's pardon

9. Three of the invitees to the gathering are:
   A. town officials
   B. teachers
   C. spiritualists

10. After leaving the kitchen, Ahineev's frame of mind is:
    A. panicky
    B. envious
    C. amused

The Story of an Hour
Kate Chopin 1894

Knowing that Mrs. Mallard was **afflicted** with a heart trouble, great care was taken to break to her as gently as possible the news of her husband's death.

It was her sister Josephine who told her, in broken sentences; veiled hints that revealed in half concealing. Her husband's friend Richards was there, too, near her. It was he who had been in the newspaper office when **intelligence** of the railroad disaster was received, with Brently Mallard's name leading the list of "killed." He had only taken the time to assure himself of its truth by a second telegram, and had hastened to **forestall** any less careful, less tender friend in bearing the sad message.

She did not hear the story as many women have heard the same, with a paralyzed inability to accept its significance. She wept at once, with sudden, wild **abandonment**, in her sister's arms. When the storm of grief had spent itself she went away to her room alone. She would have no one follow her.

There stood, facing the open window, a comfortable, roomy armchair. Into this she sank, pressed down by a physical exhaustion that haunted her body and seemed to reach into her soul.

She could see in the open square before her house the tops of trees that were all aquiver with the new spring life. The **delicious** breath of rain was in the air. In the street below a peddler was crying his wares. The notes of a distant song which some one was singing reached her faintly, and countless sparrows were twittering in the **eaves**.

There were patches of blue sky showing here and there through the clouds that had met and piled one above the other in the west facing her window.

She sat with her head thrown back upon the cushion of the chair, quite motionless, except when a sob came up into her

Kate Chopin – author considered a forerunner of feminist writers of the 20th century

afflicted – distressed or beset with mental or bodily pain

intelligence – news, knowledge

forestall – prevent or obstruct in advance

abandonment – total lack of inhibition or restraint

delicious – delightful

eaves – roof overhang

throat and shook her, as a child who has cried itself to sleep continues to sob in its dreams.

She was young, with a fair, calm face, whose lines bespoke repression and even a certain strength. But now there was a dull stare in her eyes, whose gaze was fixed away off yonder on one of those patches of blue sky. It was not a glance of reflection, but rather indicated a suspension of intelligent thought.

There was something coming to her and she was waiting for it, fearfully. What was it? She did not know; it was too subtle and **elusive** to name. But she felt it, creeping out of the sky, reaching toward her through the sounds, the scents, the color that filled the air.

elusive – difficult to find, catch, or remember

Now her bosom rose and fell tumultuously. She was beginning to recognize this thing that was approaching to possess her, and she was striving to beat it back with her will -- as powerless as her two white slender hands would have been. When she abandoned herself a little whispered word escaped her slightly parted lips. She said it over and over under her breath: "free, free, free!" The vacant stare and the look of terror that had followed it went from her eyes. They stayed keen and bright. Her pulses beat fast, and the coursing blood warmed and relaxed every inch of her body.

She did not stop to ask if it were or were not a monstrous joy that held her. A clear and exalted perception enabled her to dismiss the suggestion as trivial. She knew that she would weep again when she saw the kind, tender hands folded in death; the face that had never looked **save** with love upon her, fixed and gray and dead. But she saw beyond that bitter moment a long procession of years to come that would belong to her absolutely. And she opened and spread her arms out to them in welcome.

save – except

There would be no one to live for during those coming years; she would live for herself. There would be no powerful **will** bending hers in that blind **persistence** with which men and women believe they have a right to impose a private will upon a fellow-creature. A kind intention or a cruel intention

will – strong determination

persistence – continued existence despite difficulty or opposition

made the act seem no less a crime as she looked upon it in that brief moment of **illumination**.

And yet she had loved him -- sometimes. Often she had not. What did it matter! What could love, the unsolved mystery, count for in the face of this possession of self-assertion which she suddenly recognized as the strongest impulse of her being!

"Free! Body and soul free!" she kept whispering.

Josephine was kneeling before the closed door with her lips to the **keyhold**, **imploring** for admission. "Louise, open the door! I beg; open the door -- you will make yourself ill. What are you doing, Louise? For heaven's sake open the door."

"Go away. I am not making myself ill." No; she was drinking in a very **elixir** of life through that open window.

Her **fancy** was **running riot** along those days ahead of her. Spring days, and summer days, and all sorts of days that would be her own. She breathed a quick prayer that life might be long. It was only yesterday she had thought with a shudder that life might be long.

She arose at length and opened the door to her sister's **importunities**. There was a feverish triumph in her eyes, and she carried herself **unwittingly** like a goddess of Victory. She clasped her sister's waist, and together they descended the stairs. Richards stood waiting for them at the bottom.

Someone was opening the front door with a latchkey. It was Brently Mallard who entered, a little travel-stained, **composedly** carrying his **grip-sack** and umbrella. He had been far from the scene of the accident, and did not even know there had been one. He stood amazed at Josephine's piercing cry; at Richards' quick motion to screen him from the view of his wife.

When the doctors came they said she had died of heart disease -- of the joy that kills.

illumination – intellectual enlightenment, clarification

keyhold – keyhole

implore – beg earnestly; beseech

elixir – magical or medicinal

fancy – imagination

run riot – behave in an uncontrolled or violent way

importunity – insistent request or demand

unwitting – unknowing, unintentional

composed – calm, collected, serene

grip-sack – traveling bag

The Story of an Hour

1. The news of the railroad disaster is first received by:
   A. telegram
   B. Mrs. Mallard's sister-in-law
   C. Mr. Mallard's friend

2. Mrs. Mallard's initial reaction to the news is:
   A. emotional paralysis
   B. weeping
   C. shocked disbelief

3. Mr. Mallard is said to have treated his wife with:
   A. neglect
   B. affection
   C. indifference

4. Louise Mallard leaves her upstairs room feeling:
   A. relaxed
   B. triumphant
   C. isolated

5. The doctors conclude that Mrs. Mallard has died from great:
   A. shock
   B. upset
   C. happiness

6. The word *"elusive"* as used in the passage (¶ 9) most nearly means:
   A. penetrating
   B. slippery
   C. speedy

7. Louise "breathed a quick prayer that life may be long" because she was then feeling:
   A. gravely ill
   B. happiness might be arriving
   C. her husband would be a changed man

8. Louise first imagines her husband:
   A. in a coffin
   B. greeting and embracing her
   C. praying for her

9. Richards screens Brantly from viewing his wife because:
   A. she was tottering at the top of the stairs
   B. Brantly would be shocked at her expression
   C. her face was streaked with tears

10. This tale might best be classified as:
    A. mystery
    B. horror
    C. realistic

The Wife
Washington Irving 1819

The treasures of the deep are not so precious
As are the concealed comforts of a man
Locked up in woman's love. I scent the air
Of blessings, when I come but near the house.
What a delicious breath marriage sends forth . . .
The violet beds not sweeter.
—Thomas Middleton

I have often had occasion to remark the **fortitude** with which women sustain the most overwhelming reverses of fortune. Those disasters which break down the spirit of a man and **prostrate** him in the dust, seem to call forth all the energies of the softer sex, and give such **intrepidity** and elevation to their character that at times it approaches to **sublimity**. Nothing can be more touching than to behold a soft and tender female, who had been all weakness and dependence, and alive to every trivial roughness, while treading the prosperous paths of life, suddenly rising in mental force to be the comforter and support of her husband under misfortune, and abiding with unshrinking firmness the bitterest blasts of **adversity**.

As the vine which has long twined its graceful foliage about the oak and been lifted by it into sunshine, will, when the hardy plant is **rifted** by the thunderbolt, cling round it with its caressing tendrils and bind up its shattered boughs, so is it beautifully ordered by **Providence** that woman, who is the mere dependent and ornament of man in his happier hours, should be his stay and solace when smitten with sudden **calamity**, winding herself into the rugged recesses of his nature, tenderly supporting the drooping head, and binding up the broken heart.

I was once congratulating a friend, who had around him a blooming family, knit together in the strongest affection. "I can wish you no better **lot**," said he with enthusiasm, " than to have a wife and children. If you are prosperous, there they are to share your prosperity; if otherwise, there they are to comfort you." And indeed I have observed that a married man

Washington Irving – 19th-century American author credited with developing the short story form

fortitude – strength of mind

prostrate – lie flat, face to the ground

intrepidity – fearlessness

sublimity – of high spiritual, moral, or intellectual worth

adversity – serious difficulty or misfortune

rifted – split, cleaved

Providence – divine guidance or care

calamity – disastrous event bringing great or terrible loss or distress

lot – fate, destiny

falling into misfortune is more apt to retrieve his situation in the world than a single one; partly because he is more stimulated to exertion by the necessities of the helpless and beloved beings who depend upon him for **subsistence**; but chiefly because his spirits are soothed and relieved by domestic endearments, and his self-respect kept alive by finding, that though all abroad is darkness and humiliation, yet there is still a little world of love at home, of which he is the monarch. Whereas a single man is apt to run to waste and self-neglect; to fancy himself lonely and abandoned, and his heart to fall to ruin like some deserted mansion, for **want** of an inhabitant.

These observations call to mind a little domestic story, of which I was once a witness. My intimate friend, Leslie, had married a beautiful and accomplished girl, who had been brought up in the midst of fashionable life. She had, it is true, no fortune, but that of my friend was ample; and he delighted in the anticipation of indulging her in every elegant pursuit, and administering to those delicate tastes and **fancies** that spread a kind of witchery about the sex. "Her life," said he, "shall be like a fairy tale."

The very difference in their characters produced an harmonious combination: he was of a romantic and somewhat serious cast; she was all life and gladness. I have often noticed the mute rapture with which he would gaze upon her in company, of which her **sprightly** powers made her the delight; and how, in the midst of applause, her eye would still turn to him, as if there alone she sought favor and acceptance. When leaning on his arm, her slender form contrasted finely with his tall manly person. The fond confiding air with which she looked up to him seemed to call forth a flush of triumphant pride and cherishing tenderness, as if he doted on his lovely burden for its very helplessness. Never did a couple set forward on the flowery path of early and well-suited marriage with a fairer prospect of **felicity**.

It was the misfortune of my friend, however, to have embarked his property in large **speculations**; and he had not been married many months, when, by a succession of sudden disasters, it was swept from him, and he found himself

subsistence – remaining in existence, means of supporting life

want – lack

fancies – imagination, fantasy

sprightly – full of youthful, vibrant energy

felicity – bliss, great happiness

speculations – taking unusual business risks in hope of profit

167

reduced almost to **penury**. For a time he kept his situation to himself, and went about with a **haggard countenance** and a breaking heart. His life was but a protracted agony; and what rendered it more insupportable was the necessity of keeping up a smile in the presence of his wife; for he could not bring himself to overwhelm her with the news. She saw, however, with the quick eyes of affection, that all was not well with him. She **marked** his altered looks and stifled sighs, and was not to be deceived by his sickly and **vapid** attempts at cheerfulness. She tasked all her sprightly powers and tender **blandishments** to win him back to happiness; but she only drove the arrow deeper into his soul. The more he saw cause to love her, the more torturing was the thought that he was soon to make her wretched. "A little while," thought he, "and the smile will vanish from that cheek, the song will die away from those lips, the lustre of those eyes will be quenched with sorrow; and the happy heart, which now beats lightly in that bosom, will be weighed down like mine by the cares and miseries of the world."

At length he came to me one day, and related his whole situation in a tone of the deepest despair. When I heard him through I inquired, " Does your wife know all this?"- At the question he burst into an agony of tears. "For God's sake!" cried he, "if you have any pity on me, don't mention my wife; it is the thought of her that drives me almost to madness!"

"And why not?" said I. "She must know it sooner or later; you cannot keep it long from her, and the **intelligence** may break upon her in a more startling manner than if imparted by yourself; for the accents of those we love soften the hardest tidings. Besides, you are depriving yourself of the comforts of her sympathy; and not merely that, but also endangering the only bond that can keep hearts together an unreserved community of thought and feeling. She will soon perceive that something is secretly preying upon your mind; and true love will not **brook** reserve; it feels undervalued and outraged, when even the sorrows of those it loves are concealed from it."

"Oh, but, my friend! to think what a blow I am to give to all her future prospects--how I am to strike her very soul to the

penury – extreme want or poverty

haggard – having a gaunt, wasted, or exhausted appearance, as from prolonged suffering

countenance – face, facial expression

marked – took notice of

vapid – dull, flat, lacking liveliness

blandishments – allurements by flattery, enticements

intelligence – information, knowledge

brook – tolerate, stand for

earth, by telling her that her husband is a beggar! that she is to forego all the elegancies of life all the pleasures of society to shrink with me into **indigence** and obscurity! To tell her that I have dragged her down from the sphere in which she might have continued to move in constant brightness--the light of every eye--the admiration of every heart! How can she bear poverty? she has been brought up in all the refinements of **opulence**. How can she bear neglect? she has been the idol of society. Oh! it will break her heart it will break her heart!

I saw his grief was eloquent, and I let it have its flow; for sorrow relieves itself by words. When his **paroxysm** had subsided, and he had relapsed into moody silence, I resumed the subject gently, and urged him to break his situation at once to his wife. He shook his head mournfully, but positively.

"But how are you to keep it from her? It is necessary she should know it, that you may take the steps proper to the alteration of your circumstances. You must change your style of living--nay," observing a pang to pass across his countenance, "don't let that afflict you. I am sure you have never placed your happiness in outward show--you have yet friends, warm friends, who will not think the worse of you for being less splendidly lodged: and surely it does not require a palace to be happy with Mary."

"I could be happy with her," cried he, convulsively, "in a **hovel**! I could go down with her into poverty and the dust! I could I could, God bless her! God bless her! " cried he, bursting into a **transport** of grief and tenderness.

"And believe me, my friend," said I, stepping up and grasping him warmly by the hand, "believe me she can be the same with you. Ay, more: it will be a source of pride and triumph to her--it will call forth all the latent energies and fervent sympathies of her nature; for she will rejoice to prove that she loves you for yourself. There is in every true woman's heart a spark of heavenly fire, which lies dormant in the broad daylight of prosperity; but which kindles up, and beams and blazes in the dark hour of **adversity**. No man knows what the wife of his bosom is--no man knows what a **ministering**

indigence – extreme poverty, deprivation

opulence – wealth, riches, affluence

paroxysm – sudden or violent outburst

hovel – humble house, wretched hut

transport – strong or intense emotion, being carried away

angel she is until he has gone with her through the fiery trials of this world."

There was something in the earnestness of my manner and the figurative style of my language that caught the excited imagination of Leslie. I knew the auditor I had to deal with; and following up the impression I had made, I finished by persuading him to go home and unburden his sad heart to his wife.

I must confess, notwithstanding all I had said, I felt some little **solicitude** for the result. Who can calculate on the fortitude of one whose life has been a round of pleasures? Her gay spirits might revolt at the dark downward path of low humility suddenly pointed out before her, and might cling to the sunny regions in which they had hitherto **revelled**. Besides, ruin in fashionable life is accompanied by so many **galling mortifications**, to which in other ranks it is a stranger. In short, I could not meet Leslie the next morning without **trepidation**. He had made the disclosure.

"And how did she bear it? "

"Like an angel! It seemed rather to be a relief to her mind, for she threw her arms round my neck, and asked if this was all that had lately made me unhappy. - But, poor girl," added he, "she cannot realize the change we must undergo. She has no idea of poverty but in the abstract; she has only read of it in poetry, where it is allied to love. She feels as yet no **privation**; she suffers no loss of accustomed conveniences nor elegancies. When we come practically to experience its **sordid** cares, its **paltry** wants, its petty humiliations then will be the real trial."

"But," said I, "now that you have got over the severest task, that of breaking it to her, the sooner you let the world into the secret the better. The disclosure may be **mortifying**; but then it is a single misery, and soon over: whereas you otherwise suffer it in anticipation every hour in the day. It is not poverty so much as pretence, that harasses a ruined man--the struggle between a proud mind and an empty purse--the keeping up a hollow show that must soon come to an end. Have the

adversity – misfortune, hardship

ministering – attending to the wants of others

solicitude – attentive care and protectiveness

revelled – taken great pleasure or delight in

galling – irritating, vexing, annoying

mortifications – shame, humiliations

trepidation – fear, tremor, apprehension

privation – deprivation, lack of what is needed for existence

sordid – wretched, dirty

paltry – lacking worth, trivial

mortifying – causing shame or humiliation

170

courage to appear poor and you disarm poverty of its sharpest sting." On this point I found Leslie perfectly prepared. He had no false pride himself, and as to his wife, she was only anxious to conform to their altered fortunes.

Some days afterwards he called upon me in the evening. He had disposed of his dwelling house, and taken a small cottage in the country, a few miles from town. He had been busied all day in sending out furniture. The new establishment required few articles, and those of the simplest kind. All the splendid furniture of his late residence had been sold, excepting his wife's harp. That, he said, was too closely associated with the idea of herself; it belonged to the little story of their loves; for some of the sweetest moments of their courtship were those when he had leaned over that instrument, and listened to the melting tones of her voice. I could not but smile at this instance of romantic gallantry in a doting husband.

He was now going out to the cottage, where his wife had been all day superintending its arrangement. My feelings had become strongly interested in the progress of this family story, and as it was a fine evening, I offered to accompany him.

He was wearied with the fatigues of the day, and as he walked out, fell into a fit of gloomy musing.

"Poor Mary!" at length broke, with a heavy sigh, from his lips.

"And what of her?" asked I: "has anything happened to her?"

"What," said he, darting an impatient glance, "is it nothing to be reduced to this **paltry** situation to be caged in a miserable cottage to be obliged to toil almost in the **menial** concerns of her wretched **habitation**?"

"Has she then **repined** at the change?"

"Repined! she has been nothing but sweetness and good humor. Indeed, she seems in better spirits than I have ever

paltry – meager, inferior

menial – lowly work regarded as servile, undignified

habitation – dwelling place, home

repined – complained

171

known her; she has been to me all love and tenderness and comfort!"

"Admirable girl!" exclaimed I. "You call yourself poor, my friend; you never were so rich--you never knew the boundless treasures of excellence you possess in that woman."

"Oh! but, my friend, if this first meeting at the cottage were over, I think I could then be comfortable. But this is her first day of real experience; she has been introduced into a humble dwelling--she has been employed all day in arranging its miserable equipments--she has for the first time known the fatigues of domestic employment she has for the first time looked round her on a home **destitute** of everything elegant, almost of everything convenient; and may now be sitting down, exhausted and spiritless, brooding over a prospect of future poverty."

There was a degree of probability in this picture that I could not **gainsay**, so we walked on in silence.

After turning from the main road up a narrow lane, so thickly shaded with forest trees as to give it a complete air of seclusion, we came in sight of the cottage. It was humble enough in its appearance for the most **pastoral** poet; and yet it had a pleasing rural look. A wild vine had overrun one end with a profusion of foliage; a few trees threw their branches gracefully over it; and I observed several pots of flowers tastefully disposed about the door, and on the grass-plot in front. A small wicket gate opened upon a footpath that wound through some shrubbery to the door. Just as we approached, we heard the sound of music, Leslie grasped my arm; we paused and listened. It was Mary's voice singing, in a style of the most touching simplicity, a little **air** of which her husband was peculiarly fond.

I felt Leslie's hand tremble on my arm. He stepped forward to hear more distinctly. His step made a noise on the gravel walk. A bright beautiful face glanced out at the window and vanished--a light foot step was heard and Mary came tripping forth to meet us: she was in a pretty rural dress of white; a few wild flowers were twisted in her fine hair; a fresh bloom

destitute – suffering extreme poverty

gainsay – contradict, declare invalid, deny

pastoral – rural, suggesting idyllic country life

air – tune, song

172

was on her cheek; her whole countenance beamed with smiles--I had never seen her look so lovely.

"My dear George," cried she, "I am so glad you are come! I have been watching and watching for you; and running down the lane, and looking out for you. I've set out a table under a beautiful tree behind the cottage; and I've been gathering some of the most delicious strawberries, for I know you are fond of them and we have such excellent cream and everything is so sweet and still here. Oh!" said she, putting her arm within his, and looking up brightly in his face, "Oh, we shall be so happy!"

Poor Leslie was overcome. He caught her to his bosom--he folded his arms round her--he kissed her again and again--he could not speak, but the tears gushed into his eyes; and he has often assured me, that though the world has since gone prosperously with him, and his life has indeed been a happy one, yet never has he experienced a moment of more exquisite **felicity**.

felicity – happiness, bliss

The Wife

1. Leslie is the name of the story's:
   A. narrator
   B. heroine
   C. main character

2. The wife's husband loses his fortune through:
   A. gambling
   B. risky investments
   C. his business's bankruptcy

3. The narrator believes that in tough times:
   A. husbands try to cover up
   B. a marriage is likely to fail
   C. wives act tougher than husbands

4. In the last scene, the wife announces her:
   A. dream of a baby
   B. hopefulness
   C. happiness

5. The wife gives George a:
   A. hug
   B. dessert
   C. compliment

6. The word *"repine"* (third to last page) as used in the passage most nearly means:
   A. sigh
   B. show discontent
   C. lie back

7. The "sharpest sting" of poverty (p. 171) is said to be:
   A. to appear poor
   B. to have an unsupportive wife
   C. to have to change one's life

8. The only non-essential thing Leslie does not sell or dispose of is:
   A. their fancy bed
   B. their dog
   C. Mary's harp

9. In the story's opening poem, the view of marriage Thomas Middleton presents is:
   A. anti-feminist
   B. sentimental
   C. realistic

10. By the end of the story, Leslie is:
   A. resigned to poverty
   B. in improved financial shape
   C. the happiest ever in his life

The Wolf & the Seven Young Kids
The Brothers Grimm (1812)

Once upon a time there was an old goat. She had seven little **kids**, and loved them all, just as a mother loves her children. One day she wanted to go into the woods to get some food. So she called all seven to her and said, "Children dear, I am going into the woods. Be on your guard for the wolf. If he gets in, he will eat up all of you all, even your skin and hair. The villain often disguises himself, but you will recognize him at once by his rough voice and his black feet."

The kids said, "Mother dear, we will take care of ourselves. You can go away without any worries."

Then the old one bleated, and went on her way with her mind at ease.

It was not long before someone knocked at the door and called out, "Open the door, children dear, your mother is here, and has brought something for each one of you."

But the little kids knew from the rough voice that it was the wolf.

"We will not open the door," they cried out. "You are not our mother. She has a soft and gentle voice, but your voice is rough. You are the wolf."

So the wolf went to a shopkeeper and bought himself a large piece of chalk, which he ate, making his voice soft. Then he came back and knocked at the door, calling out, "Open the door, children dear. Your mother is here and has brought something for each one of you."

But the wolf laid one of his black paws inside the window. The children saw it and cried out, "We will not open the door. Our mother does not have a black foot like you. You are the wolf."

So the wolf ran to a baker and said, "I have sprained my foot. Rub some dough on it for me." After the baker had rubbed

Jacob and Wilhelm Grimm – 19th-century German brothers who collected and published folklore and fairy tales

kids – young goats

dough on his foot, the wolf ran to the miller and said, "Sprinkle some white flour on my foot for me."

The miller thought, "The wolf wants to deceive someone," and refused to do it, so the wolf said, "If you will not do it, I will eat you up." That frightened the miller, and he made his paw white for him. Yes, that is the way people are.

Now the villain went for a third time to the door, knocked at it, and said, "Open the door for me, children. Your dear little mother has come home, and has brought every one of you something from the woods."

The little kids cried out, "First show us your paw so we may know that you are our dear little mother."

So he put his paw inside the window, and when they saw that it was white, they believed that everything he said was true, and they opened the door. But who came in? It was the wolf. They were terrified and wanted to hide. One jumped under the table, the second into the bed, the third into the stove, the fourth into the kitchen, the fifth into the cupboard, the sixth under the washbasin, and the seventh into the **clock case**. But the wolf found them all, and with no further ado he swallowed them down his throat, one after the other. However, he did not find the youngest kid, the one who was in the clock case.

clock case – a wooden cabinet containing a pendulum clock tall enough to stand on the floor

After satisfying his appetite he went outside and lay down under a tree in the green meadow and fell asleep.

Soon afterward the old goat came home from the woods. Oh, what a sight she saw there. The door stood wide open. Table, chairs, and benches were tipped over. The **washbasin** was in pieces. The covers and pillows had been pulled off the bed. She looked for her children, but they were nowhere to be found. She called them by name, one after the other, but no one answered. When she at last came to the youngest, a soft voice cried out, "Mother dear, I am hiding in the clock case. She took it out, and it told her that the wolf had come and had

washbasin – a large bowl used for washing one's hands and face, etc.

eaten up all the others. You can just imagine how she cried for her poor children.

Finally in her despair she went outside, and the youngest kid ran with her. They came to the meadow, and there lay the wolf by the tree, snoring so loudly that the branches shook. She looked at him from all sides and saw that something was moving and jiggling inside his full belly.

"Good gracious," she thought. "Is it possible that my poor children, whom he has swallowed down for his supper, can still be alive?"

The mother goat sent the kid home and to fetch scissors, and a needle and thread, and then she cut open the monster's **paunch**. She had scarcely made one cut, before a little kid stuck its head out, and as she continued to cut, one after the other all six jumped out, and they were all still alive. They were not even hurt, for in his greed the monster had swallowed them down whole. How happy they were! They hugged their dear mother, and jumped about like a tailor on his wedding day.

paunch – pot-belly, protruding belly

But the mother said, "Go now and look for some big stones. We will fill the godless beast's stomach with them while he is still asleep."

The seven kids quickly brought the stones, and they put as many of them into his stomach as it would hold. Then the mother hurriedly sewed him up again. He was not aware of anything and never once stirred.

The wolf finally awoke and got up onto his legs. Because the stones in his stomach made him very thirsty, he wanted to go to a well and get a drink. But when he began to walk and to move about, the stones in his stomach knocked against each other and rattled.

Then he cried out:

What rumbles and tumbles,
Inside of me.

177

I thought it was kids,
But it's stones that they be.

When he got to the well and leaned over the water to drink, the heavy stones pulled him in, and he drowned miserably.

When the seven kids saw what had happened, they ran up and cried out, "The wolf is dead! The wolf is dead!" And with their mother they danced for joy around about the well.

The Wolf & the Seven Young Kids

1. The wolf is said to be recognizable by his:
    A. voice
    B. snout
    C. ears

2. The mother leaves to go into the woods to fetch:
    A. firewood
    B. food
    C. their kinfolk

3. The wolf procures chalk to change his:
    A. voice
    B. complexion
    C. paws

4. The wolf does not move when the old goat arrives and cuts open the wolf's belly because the wolf is:
    A. weighted down
    B. fatigued from eating
    C. sleeping

5. The stones in his belly made the wolf:
    A. angry
    B. wobbly
    C. thirsty

6. The mother rescues six of her kids from:
    A. a clock case
    B. the wolf's belly
    C. under a bed

7. The miller at first refuses to help the wolf, but then does because the miller:
    A. recognizes the wolf
    B. fears for his life
    C. is quite insistent

8. The six kids jump out of the wolf's belly unharmed because the wolf:
    A. hasn't chewed them
    B. already had a full belly
    C. had already eaten all the food in their house

9. The youngest kid has avoided being swallowed by:
    A. hiding
    B. being too small to bother with
    C. escaping into the woods

10. The wolf asks for some dough in order to use it to:
    A. lure the seven kids with baked cookies
    B. to soothe a sprained foot
    C. to disguise his face

179

On Women's Right to Vote
Susan B. Anthony 1872

In the 1800s, women in the United States had few legal rights and did not have the right to vote. This speech was given by Susan B. Anthony after her arrest for casting an illegal vote in the presidential election of 1872. She was tried and then fined $100 but refused to pay.

Friends and fellow citizens: I stand before you tonight under **indictment** for the alleged crime of having voted at the last presidential election, without having a lawful right to vote. It shall be my work this evening to prove to you that in thus voting, I not only committed no crime, but, instead, simply exercised my citizen's rights, guaranteed to me and all United States citizens by the National Constitution, beyond the power of any state to deny.

The **preamble** of the Federal Constitution says:

"We, the people of the United States, in order to form a more perfect union, establish justice, insure domestic **tranquility** provide for the common defense, promote the general welfare, and secure the blessings of liberty to ourselves and our **posterity**, do **ordain** and establish this Constitution for the United States of America."

It was we, the people; not we, the white male citizens; nor yet we, the male citizens; but we, the whole people, who formed the Union. And we formed it, not to give the blessings of liberty, but to secure them; not to the half of ourselves and the half of our posterity, but to the whole people - women as well as men. And it is a downright mockery to talk to women of their enjoyment of the blessings of liberty while they are denied the use of the only means of securing them provided by this democratic-republican government - the ballot.

For any state to make sex a qualification that must ever result in the **disfranchisement** of one entire half of the people, is to pass a **bill of attainder**, or, an *ex post facto* law, and is therefore a violation of the supreme law of the land. By

Susan B. Anthony – American social reformer who played a key role in the women's suffrage (voting rights) movement

indictment – a formal charge or accusation of a serious crime

preamble – an introduction to a formal document or statement explaining its purpose

tranquility – calmness, serenity, peacefulness

posterity – future generations, offspring

ordain – decree, order officially

disenfranchisement – deprivation of rights, especially right to vote

bill of attainder – a law that punishes a group or individual without trial

ex post facto – refers to a law applying "after the fact"; **i.e.** (**id est**: that is), criminalizing formerly legal conduct retroactively

it the blessings of liberty are forever withheld from women and their female posterity.

To them this government has no just powers derived from the consent of the governed. To them this government is not a democracy. It is not a republic. It is an **odious** aristocracy; a hateful **oligarchy** of sex; the most hateful aristocracy ever established on the face of the globe; an oligarchy of wealth, where the rich govern the poor. An oligarchy of learning, where the educated govern the ignorant, or even an oligarchy of race, where the Saxon rules the African, might be endured; but this oligarchy of sex, which makes father, brothers, husband, sons, the oligarchs over the mother and sisters, the wife and daughters, of every household - which ordains all men sovereigns, all women subjects, carries dissension, discord, and rebellion into every home of the nation.

Webster, Worcester, and Bouvier all define a citizen to be a person in the United States, entitled to vote and hold office.

The only question left to be settled now is: Are women persons? And I hardly believe any of our opponents will have the **hardihood** to say they are not. Being persons, then, women are citizens; and no state has a right to make any law, or to enforce any old law, that shall **abridge** their privileges or **immunities**. Hence, every discrimination against women in the constitutions and laws of the several states is today **null and void**, precisely as is every one against Negroes.

odious – hateful, offensive

oligarchy – government by a select few

hardihood – boldness and daring

abridge – reduce, curtail, shorten

immunities – protections, exemptions

null and void – with no legal force; without effect; unenforceable

Women's Right to Vote

1. The speaker was arrested for:
   A. an unpaid fine
   B. libel
   C. casting a ballot

2. Her argument is based on interpretation of the Preamble to the Constitution's word:
   A. equal
   B. men
   C. people

3. The speech says of "the blessings of liberty" that they are:
   A. based on sex
   B. implied
   C. unlegislated

4. Anthony describes the current government as:
   A. semi-democratic
   B. republican
   C. aristocratic

5. Anthony claims that those who formed the Union were:
   A. the whole people
   B. male citizens
   C. white male citizens

6. The word *"indictment"* (¶ 1) as used in the passage most nearly means:
   A. condemnation
   B. accusation
   C. criticism

7. The word "suffrage" means:
   A. tolerance
   B. permission
   C. voting rights

8. Anthony claims that ultimately one "secures the (denied) blessings of liberty" through:
   A. protest
   B. group solidarity
   C. the ballot

9. Anthony concludes that:
   A. Negroes are persons
   B. women have immunity
   C. men are in fact the weaker sex

10. The speech claims that "the oligarchy of sex" promotes:
   A. rebellion
   B. immorality
   C. civil rights

Young Benjamin Franklin
Nathaniel Hawthorne

When Benjamin Franklin was a boy he was very fond of fishing; and many of his leisure hours were spent on the margin of the mill pond catching flounders, perch, and eels that came up thither with the tide.

The place where Ben and his playmates did most of their fishing was a marshy spot on the outskirts of Boston. On the edge of the water there was a deep bed of clay, in which the boys were forced to stand while they caught their fish.

"This is very uncomfortable," said Ben Franklin one day to his comrades, while they were standing in the **quagmire**.

"So it is," said the other boys. "What a pity we have no better place to stand on!"

On the dry land, not far from the quagmire, there were at that time a great many large stones that had been brought there to be used in building the foundation of a new house. Ben mounted upon the highest of these stones.

"Boys," said he, "I have thought of a plan. You know what a plague it is to have to stand in the quagmire yonder. See, I am **bedaubed** to the knees, and you are all in the same **plight**.

"Now I propose that we build a wharf. You see these stones? The workmen mean to use them for building a house here. My plan is to take these same stones, carry them to the edge of the water, and build a wharf with them. What say you, lads? Shall we build the wharf?"

"Yes, yes," cried the boys; "let's set about it!"

It was agreed that they should all be on the spot that evening, and begin their grand public **enterprise** by moonlight.

Accordingly, at the appointed time, the boys met and eagerly began to remove the stones. They worked like a colony of ants, sometimes two or three of them taking hold of one

Nathaniel Hawthorne – American novelist and short story writer, born in 1804 in Salem, Massachusetts

quagmire – miry or boggy ground whose surface gives way underfoot

bedaubed – smeared with a thick or sticky substance

plight – dangerous or difficult situation

enterprise – project involving boldness or effort

stone; and at last they had carried them all away, and built their little wharf.

"Now, boys," cried Ben, when the job was done, "let's give three cheers, and go home to bed. To-morrow we may catch fish at our ease."

"Hurrah! hurrah! hurrah!" shouted his comrades, and all scampered off home and to bed, to dream of to-morrow's sport.

In the morning the **masons** came to begin their work. But what was their surprise to find the stones all gone! The master mason, looking carefully on the ground, saw the tracks of many little feet, some with shoes and some barefoot. Following these to the water side, he soon found what had become of the missing building stones.

masons – stone workers

"Ah! I see what the mischief is," said he; "those little rascals who were here yesterday have stolen the stones to build a wharf with. And I must say that they understand their business well."

He was so angry that he at once went to make a complaint before the **magistrate**; and his Honor wrote an order to "take the bodies of Benjamin Franklin, and other evil-disposed persons," who had stolen a heap of stones.

magistrate – minor judicial officer, official with administrative and often judicial functions

If the owner of the stolen property had not been more merciful than the master mason, it might have gone hard with our friend Benjamin and his comrades. But, luckily for them, the gentleman had a respect for Ben's father, and, moreover, was pleased with the spirit of the whole affair. He therefore let the culprits off easily.

But the poor boys had to go through another **trial**, and receive sentence, and suffer punishment, too, from their own fathers. Many a **rod** was worn to the stump on that unlucky night. As for Ben, he was less afraid of a whipping than of his father's **reproof**. And, indeed, his father was very much disturbed.

trial – examination of blame or guilt

rod – stick used for punishment

"Benjamin, come hither," began Mr. Franklin in his usual stern and weighty tone. The boy approached and stood before his father's chair. "Benjamin," said his father, "what could induce you to take property which did not belong to you?"

reproof – rebuke, criticism, blame

verily – truly, indeed

"Why, father," replied Ben, hanging his head at first, but then lifting his eyes to Mr. Franklin's face, "if it had been merely for my own benefit, I never should have dreamed of it. But I knew that the wharf would be a public convenience. If the owner of the stones should build a house with them, nobody would enjoy any advantage but himself. Now, I made use of them in a way that was for the advantage of many persons."

"My son," said Mr. Franklin solemnly, "so far as it was in your power, you have done a greater harm to the public than to the owner of the stones. I do **verily** believe, Benjamin, that almost all the public and private misery of mankind arises from a neglect of this great truth,--that evil can produce only evil, that good ends must be wrought out by good means."

To the end of his life, Ben Franklin never forgot this conversation with his father; and we have reason to suppose, that, in most of his public and private career, he sought to act upon the principles which that good and wise man then taught him.

Young Benjamin Franklin

1. Franklin and his friends intend to build a:
   A. stone wall
   B. pier
   C. fort

2. The boys begin their work in the evening because:
   A. the land is private property
   B. the rocks are stolen
   C. it's too hot to work during the day

3. The master mason reacts to the boys' work with:
   A. anger
   B. amusement
   C. admiration

4. The boys are punished by:
   A. the magistrate
   B. the property owner
   C. their elders

5. Mr. Franklin views the boys' construction as:
   A. a public benefit
   B. a public harm
   C. juvenile mischief

6. The narrative takes place near:
   A. Philadelphia
   B. Boston
   C. New York

7. Ben's father is portrayed as:
   A. moralizing
   B. fair
   C. forgiving

8. Ben's explanation of the stone construction as a "public convenience" (p. 185) shows:
   A. his belief in public service
   B. his ability to rationalize
   C. his idealism

9. The person who is most pleased at what Ben has accomplished is:
   A. the stone mason
   B. the stones' owner
   C. Ben's father

10. The stones were intended for a:
    A. school
    B. breakwater
    C. house

Answer Key

	1	2	3	4	5		6	7	8	9	10
Albert Einstein's Letter to FDR	B	B	C	B	C		A	B	A	A	B
Burning of Washington	B	B	C	A	C		C	C	B	B	B
Canterbury Tales: Prologue	B	B	C	B	A		C	B	A	A	C
Captain Murderer	C	C	B	C	A		C	C	A	A	C
Celebrated Jumping Frog	A	A	A	C	A		B	B	A	C	B
Cheshire Cat	B	C	C	C	C		C	B	B	C	B
Clean Well-Lighted Place	C	B	A	C	A		B	C	C	B	A
Code of Hammurabi	C	C	A	B	B		A	C	C	C	B
Death of Socrates	C	B	C	C	A		C	A	A	A	A
Death of the Moth	A	C	C	A	C		A	A	C	A	C
Destiny of Colored Americans	C	A	A	B	A		B	C	A	C	A
Diary of Anne Frank	B	C	B	B	A		B	C	B	B	A
Discovery of Radium	A	C	A	B	B		A	C	B	A	A
Eisenhower Farewell Address	B	A	C	B	C		B	B	C	B	B
Faulkner's Nobel Speech	C	C	A	B	A		B	B	C	C	C
Faust	C	A	A	C	C		A	C	A	A	C
Geronimo Speech	A	C	C	A	B		A	A	C	A	B
Gift of the Magi	A	A	B	C	C		C	A	B	A	C
Gladiators	B	C	A	A	C		C	C	B	C	B

	1	*2*	*3*	*4*	*5*		*6*	*7*	*8*	*9*	*10*
John Brown's Final Words	B	A	A	B	C		C	C	A	B	A
Lady, or the Tiger?	C	C	C	A	B		A	A	B	A	B
Letter from Hernan Cortez	A	C	B	B	B		C	C	B	B	C
Liberty or Death	B	B	A	C	B		C	A	B	C	B
Lincoln's Second Inaugaral	B	B	B	A	C		C	A	C	B	C
Little Match Seller	A	C	C	C	A		B	B	C	B	A
Mass of Shadows	A	C	A	A	B		C	C	B	B	A
Of Studies	B	B	C	A	B		B	C	B	A	C
Open Window	B	C	C	A	A		B	A	A	B	B
Oval Portrait	C	A	C	A	A		C	A	A	A	B
Present at Hanging	C	A	B	C	C		C	C	C	A	B
Procuring Pleasant Dreams	A	A	C	B	B		A	B	B	B	A
Prodigal Son	C	B	B	B	A		B	B	B	C	C
Scott's Last Diary Entries	B	C	C	C	B		C	C	B	C	C
Secret Life of Walter Mitty	B	A	C	B	C		B	B	B	A	B
Slander	C	A	C	A	C		A	A	A	B	A
Story of an Hour	C	B	B	B	C		A	A	B	B	A
Wife	A	B	C	C	B		B	A	C	B	B

	1	2	3	4	5	6	7	8	9	10
Wolf & the Seven Young Kids	A	B	C	C	C	B	B	A	A	B
Women's Right to Vote	C	C	A	C	A	B	C	C	A	A
Young Benjamin Franklin	B	B	A	C	B	B	A	B	B	C